I0012700

Vue.js
100 Interview Questions

X.Y. Wang

Contents

3

3 Intermediate 43

4 Advanced   75

6 Master 147

Chapter 1

Preface

In the ever-evolving landscape of web development, Vue.js has emerged as a beacon of flexibility, simplicity, and power. Its rise to prominence is not just a testament to its capabilities, but also to the community that has embraced, nurtured, and propelled it to the forefront of modern web frameworks. As Vue.js continues to gain traction, the demand for proficient developers in this domain has surged, leading to a pressing need for resources that can guide, train, and evaluate one's knowledge of Vue.js.

"Vue.js: 100 Interview Questions" is not just a book; it's a journey. A journey that takes you from the foundational concepts of Vue.js to the intricate nuances that only seasoned developers are familiar with. Whether you're a beginner looking to start your Vue journey, an intermediate developer aiming to solidify your understanding, or an expert seeking to delve into the framework's deepest recesses, this book is tailored for you.

The structure of this book is meticulously designed to mirror the progression of a Vue developer. Starting with basic questions, it gently introduces the core concepts, ensuring a solid foundation. As you progress, the questions become more challenging, pushing you to explore and understand the more advanced features and best practices of Vue.js. By the time you reach the 'Master' section, you'll be delving into architectural decisions, advanced patterns, and nuanced aspects that few have ventured into.

But why focus on interview questions? Interviews are unique in that they not only test knowledge but also one's ability to articulate, reason, and sometimes even teach. By framing this book around interview questions, we aim to prepare you not just for job interviews, but also for real-world scenarios where understanding and communication are paramount.

Lastly, I'd like to extend my gratitude to the Vue.js community. This book is a culmination of countless experiences, discussions, and lessons learned from developers around the world. It's a testament to the collaborative spirit of the open-source world, and I'm honored to contribute to it.

As you turn the pages, I hope this book challenges you, enlightens you, and above all, fuels your passion for Vue.js. Here's to a journey of discovery, learning, and growth.

Chapter 2

Basic

2.1 What is Vue.js?

Vue.js is a progressive JavaScript framework, developed by Evan You, used for building user interfaces, specifically for single-page applications. The core of Vue.js is mainly focused on what is referred to as the view layer of an application. This aligns with its goal to be used incrementally, meaning that it can be adopted into an existing codebase gradually.

The term "progressive" used to describe Vue.js refers to the framework's design which allows for developers to add as much or as little of Vue.js to their projects as needed. If you need to add a bit of Vue.js for a few dynamic widgets being added to an existing page, it is very simple to do so without having to re-architect your entire project.

Vue.js has an adaptable architecture that focuses on declarative rendering and component composition which makes it easy to understand and also easy to integrate with existing projects. It's also incredibly robust for building complex single-page applications when used in conjunction with modern tools and supporting libraries.

A basic Vue.js application may look something like this:

```
var app = new Vue({
  el: '#app',
  data: {
    message: 'Hello Vue!'
  }
})
```

Here, we're creating a new Vue instance and passing an options object. The "el" option tells Vue which element the instance should be mounted on. In this case, we're targeting the element with the id "app". In the "data" object, we have our application state, and we're just starting with a single "message" property.

When we want to display the state inside the HTML, we use the double curly brace syntax for "text interpolation".

```
<div id="app">
  <p>{{ message }}</p>
</div>
```

The Vue instance takes an object of options, which can include data, template, el, methods, life cycle hooks, etc. Vue uses a DOM-based templating system, so all the Vue templates are valid HTML that can be parsed by spec-compliant browsers and HTML parsers.

2.2   How do you set up a new Vue project?

Setting up a new Vue project is quite straightforward with Vue CLI (Command Line Interface). Below are the steps to create a new project in Vue.js:

1. First, you have to install Node.js and npm. Node.js is a Javascript runtime that executes Javascript code outside of a web browser. You can download the latest version of Node.js from their official website. npm is a package manager for Javascript, which is automatically installed when you install Node.js.

2. Once you have Node.js and npm installed, you can install Vue CLI globally on your computer by running the following command in your terminal:

```
npm install -g @vue/cli
```

If you have previously installed Vue CLI (version 2.x), you should uninstall it first by running 'npm uninstall vue-cli -g' in the terminal, then install the new Vue CLI.

3. Now, you're ready to create a new Vue.js project. Navigate to the directory where you want to create your project and run the following command:

```
vue create my-project
```

Make sure to replace "my-project" with the name you want for your project.

4. This command will prompt you with project configurations. For a beginner, it's recommended to choose the "default preset" which includes a proper configuration of Babel and ESLint.

5. Once you've selected your preset, Vue CLI will create and initialize your project. When the setup is complete, navigate to your project directory by running 'cd my-project'.

6. With all the setup completed, you can now start your Vue.js application by running:

```
npm run serve
```

This will compile your application and run it on a local server. You can access your app by opening a web browser and navigating to localhost:8080 (or your specified port number).

By following these steps, you have successfully set up a new Vue project on your development environment.

2.3   What is the Vue instance and what is its purpose?

In Vue.js, every application starts by creating a new Vue instance with the 'Vue' function:

```
var vm = new Vue({
  // options
})
```

The Vue instance is the heart of every Vue application. It connects the Vue library to an element in your HTML and thus allows you to create a reactive link between the Vue instance's data object and your HTML, enabling you to dynamically manipulate the Document Object Model (DOM).

A Vue instance accepts an options object, which can include several directives or options. Some of these include:

1. The 'el' option: This is an element in the DOM that the Vue instance will be attached to. It can be specified as a CSS selector string or an actual HTMLElement.

2. The 'data' option: This option contains the data that you want to keep track of within this Vue instance.

3. The 'methods' option: This option contains the methods that you want to use within this Vue instance.

4. Other options such as 'computed', 'watch', 'props', 'components' etc.

Here's an illustration of how to create a Vue instance:

```
var vm = new Vue({
  el: '#app',
  data: {
    message: 'Hello World!',
  },
  methods: {
    hello: function() {
      return this.message;
```

```
    },
  },
});
```

In the example above, we created a new Vue instance and attached it to the HTML element with the id of 'app'. We've also tracked a piece of data, 'message', and created a method 'hello'. This allows us to display the 'message' on the webpage, and the method 'hello' is usable within the instance's scope.

With Vue instances, manipulating and interacting with HTML in a reactive way becomes easier and more intuitive.

2.4 Explain the Vue.js lifecycle. Name some of its hooks.

The Vue.js lifecycle is a series of steps that Vue.js goes through when creating, updating, and removing a component. Here are the hooks in the order they are invoked:

1. **beforeCreate:** The beforeCreate life-cycle hook runs before instance creation, hence you will not be able to access reactive data and events, as they have not been initialized yet.

2. **created:** If you need to access reactive data or events inside this hook, this is the most appropriate place to do it.

3. **beforeMount:** The beforeMount hook runs right before the initial render happens and after the template or render functions have been compiled.

4. **mounted:** The mounted hook runs after the initial render. When this hook runs, the component has been created and inserted into the DOM.

5. **beforeUpdate:** When you need to get the new state, you will

have to wait for Vue.js to update the DOM first, which is when computed properties and watchers will re-render based on this updated state.

6. **updated:** This life cycle hook is called after a data change causes the virtual DOM to be re-rendered and patched.

7. **beforeDestroy:** This hook runs right before tearing down the instance.

8. **destroyed:** Finally the destroyed hook runs after tearing down the instance. Most of the cleanup tasks like, clearing timers or cleaning up event listeners should be done in this hook.

This Vue.js lifecycle might be represented in pseudo-code as follows:

```
new Vue({
  data() {
    return {
      message: 'Hello, World!'
    }
  },
  beforeCreate() {
    // Code before instance is created
  },
  created() {
    // Code after instance is created
  },
  beforeMount() {
    // Code before initial render
  },
  mounted() {
    // Code after initial render
  },
  beforeUpdate() {
    // Code before update
  },
  updated() {
    // Code after update
  },
  beforeDestroy() {
    // Code before instance is destroyed
  },
  destroyed() {
    // Code after instance is destroyed
  }
})
```

The Vue.js lifecycle allows developers to add their own code at different stages of the component. For instance, the created hook can be used to run code after an instance is created. Examples include fetching data for your component (possibly using AJAX) and storing it in your data values.

2.5 How do you bind data to a template in Vue?

Data binding in Vue.js is accomplished via a system of directives that are pre-set HTML attributes. These directives are how Vue.js is able to dynamically add content to an HTML file. The syntax is quite simple: just add "v-" to the beginning of an HTML attribute.

The directive for data binding in Vue.js is "v-bind". It lets you re-actively bind an attribute to an expression. If the expression's value changes, the attribute's value updates to reflect the change.

For example, let's say we want to dynamically bind the href attribute of an anchor tag. Here is how you would do it in Vue:

```
<template>
  <div>
    <a v-bind:href="url">Vue.js Documentation</a>
  </div>
</template>

<script>
export default {
  data() {
    return {
      url: "https://vuejs.org/v2/guide/"
    };
  }
};
</script>
```

In the example above, Vue will replace the 'href' attribute of the anchor tag with the value of 'url' from the component's data properties.

An even simpler way to bind data to attribute is with the shorthand syntax, which involves removing the v-bind part and just using the colon ":". Here's the same example with the shorthand:

```
<template>
  <div>
    <a :href="url">Vue.js Documentation</a>
  </div>
</template>
```

Another fundamental way to bind data to a template is using the
mustache syntax " ". This is for rendering the text content. If we use
the above example, it will like:

```
<template>
  <div>
    <p>URL is: {{ url }}</p>
  </div>
</template>
```

In the example above, Vue will replace the 'URL is: url ' with the
value of 'url' from the component's data properties. It's important to
mention that the double mustache syntax can only be used in HTML
content. It won't work for HTML attributes. For these cases, you
will have to use the v-bind directive, or its shorthand ":".

2.6   What is the difference between v-bind and v-model?

'v-bind' and 'v-model' are two Vue.js directives that are used to bind
data from Vue instances to HTML elements. There are some differences in how they are used and how they function.

'v-bind': This directive is used to bind one or multiple attributes, or
a component prop to an expression. When its expression changes, the
value of the bound attribute / prop will change accordingly. It can
be used with any attribute (class, style, etc.) of an HTML tag. For
example:

```
<input v-bind:value="message" />
```

In this example, 'message' is a Vue data property. Whenever the 'message' property changes, the value attribute of this input tag will also change.

'v-model': It is a two-way data binding directive. It binds the view into the model, and the model into the view. This is useful when you want to handle input field data within Vue.js. For example:

```
<input v-model="message" />
```

In the case of 'v-model', it not only changes the value of the input field when the 'message' property changes, but it also changes the value of the 'message' property when the input field changes. This is why we say 'v-model' provides two-way data binding.

To sum it up, you can use 'v-bind' when you want to bind a value to a property of an element and don't need to change it or get the value back from the element. You use 'v-model' for input fields where you usually want to both display a value and get the value back after user input.

2.7 How do you conditionally render elements in Vue?

Conditionally rendering elements in Vue.js is achieved using the 'v-if', 'v-else-if' and 'v-else' directives. Vue.js adds or removes elements depending on the truthiness of the expression in the directive.

1. 'v-if': This directive is used to conditionally render a block. The block will only be rendered if the directive's expression returns a truthy value.

```
<div v-if="isVisible">This will be visible if the 'isVisible' expression is
    truthy</div>
```

In this example, the 'div' will only be rendered in the DOM if 'isVisible' is truthy. If 'isVisible' is false, the 'div' will not be included in the render tree at all.

2. 'v-else': This is the companion directive for 'v-if'. Its use is very similar in pattern to 'else' in JavaScript conditional branching.

```
<div v-if="isVisible">If condition</div>
<div v-else>Else condition</div>
```

In this example, if the 'isVisible' variable is truthy, the first 'div' will be rendered. If 'isVisible' is falsy, then the second 'div' (with the 'v-else' directive) will be rendered instead.

3. 'v-else-if': This directive is used when you want to add an 'else if' condition. It can be chained multiple times.

```
<div v-if="value ===  'A'">Value is A</div>
<div v-else-if="value ===  'B'">Value is B</div>
<div v-else>Value is neither A nor B</div>
```

In this example, depending on the value of the variable 'value', different messages will be rendered.

Keep in mind that Vue.js compiles template directives like 'v-if' and 'v-else' at render time and that using them can lead to the creation and destruction of instances which may have an impact on performance. For cases where elements are frequently shown and hidden, using 'v-show' (which toggles the CSS 'display' property instead of destroying and recreating instances) can be more efficient.

2.8   How do you loop through lists in Vue templates?

In Vue.js, you loop through lists using the 'v-for' directive. This directive is used for rendering lists. It works in conjunction with an HTML template or component to iterate over a list of items, where upon each iteration, it generates a new template or component instance and binds the item to that instance.

Here is a basic example:

```
<ul id="example-1">
  <li v-for="item␣in␣items">{{ item.message }}</li>
</ul>

var vm = new Vue({
  el: '#example-1',
  data: {
    items: [
      { message: 'Foo' },
      { message: 'Bar' }
    ]
  }
})
```

In this case, 'v-for' iterates over the 'items' array and for each item, it creates and renders a new '<li>' HTML element. It also binds each item to the newly created element. Therefore, two list items with the text 'Foo' and 'Bar' will be created.

Additionally, you have access to the current array index during iteration by providing a second argument to 'v-for':

```
<ul id="example-2">
  <li v-for="(item,␣index)␣in␣items">{{ index }} - {{ item.message }}</li>
</ul>
```

This example will output the item's index in the list plus the item's message.

Lastly, 'v-for' directive is also capable of iterating over an object's properties:

```
<ul id="example-3">
  <li v-for="value␣in␣object">
    {{ value }}
  </li>
</ul>

var vm = new Vue({
  el: '#example-3',
  data: {
    object: {
      firstName: 'John',
      lastName: 'Doe',
      age: 30
    }
  }
})
```

The above example will render a list of the object's values, in this case 'John', 'Doe', and '30'. If you want both the key and value of object properties, you would use '(value, key)' in 'v-for'.

2.9 What is a Vue component? How do you create one?

A Vue.js component is a reusable, self-contained block of code that encapsulates HTML, CSS, and JavaScript functionalities that can be used to construct an application's user interface. Components are versatile and reusable Vue instances with a name. The idea is similar to JavaScript functions, where we can define a function once and use it in many places.

There are several ways to define a Vue component, but the most common is using Vue.component() method. Here's an example:

```
Vue.component('my-component-name', {
  // options
})
```

In the above example, we have created a Vue component called 'my-component-name'.

Now let's take a look at a more concrete example. In this case, the component is used to render a button with a specific behavior:

```
Vue.component('my-button', {
  data: function () {
    return {
      count: 0
    }
  },
  template: '<button v-on:click="count++">You clicked me {{ count }} times.</
      button>'
})
```

This example lifts the burden of adding event listeners and manipulating the DOM off of the developer and entrusts Vue.js with the task of updating the app's UI.

The options object in the Vue.component() method takes several properties such as data, methods, computed, watcher, props, etc. For instance, data is used to store the variables, methods to store the methods, computed to store the computed properties, and so on.

Later on, when we create a new Vue instance, we can use this component as a custom element inside our root Vue instance's template:

```
<div id="app">
    <my-button></my-button>
</div>

new Vue({ el: '#app' })
```

Vue components are the fundamental building blocks of Vue.js applications. They provide a system for defining reusable and encapsulated JavaScript functions and organizing an application's user interface into a hierarchy of nested, reusable chunks.

2.10 How do you pass data from a parent component to a child component?

In Vue.js, you can pass data from a parent component to a child component through the use of props. In Vue.js, the parent component can pass data down to child components through props, which are custom attributes you can register on a component.

Here's a basic example to illustrate:

```
// Parent component
Vue.component('parent-component', {
  template: '<child-component␣:my-prop="parentData"></child-component>',
  data: function() {
    return {
      parentData: 'Hello␣World'
    }
  }
})

// Child component
Vue.component('child-component', {
  props: ['myProp'],
  template: '<div>{{␣myProp␣}}</div>'
```

```
})
```

In the above example, 'parentData' is a data property in the parent component and it is passed down to a prop ('myProp') in the child component. Notably, ':myProp' is a shorthand for binding in Vue.js syntax, which is equivalent to 'v-bind:myProp'.

In the child component definition, you see 'props: ['myProp']'. This tells Vue that this component expects a 'myProp' attribute in its element and it should bind it locally in its scope.

In the parent component's template, '<child-component :my-prop= "parentData">' binds 'parentData' to 'myProp'. The value of 'parentData' from the parent is then passed as a prop to the child component.

When the child component then gets rendered, it would use the received 'myProp' data to render the 'div' element. In the example above, the child component would render a 'div' with the content 'Hello World'.

2.11   What are Vue.js directives? Name a few.

Vue.js directives are special attributes with the 'v-' prefix that are expected to be used on the View layer of the Vue.js application.

They add special reactive behavior to the rendered DOM. This means they can change the output based on the changes to Vue instances. Basically, directives are the building blocks of any Vue.js application because almost anything that you do in Vue involves directives.

Here are a few Vue.js directives:

1. **v-bind**: This directive helps you to bind an attribute of an HTML element to an expression or a property of the Vue instance.

One common use case is binding the 'src' attribute of an 'img' tag to a property.

```
<img v-bind:src="imageUrl">
```

2. **v-on**: It is used to listen to DOM events and execute some JavaScript code when they're triggered.

```
<button v-on:click="add">Increment</button>
```

3. **v-if, v-else and v-else-if**: These three directives are used for conditional rendering. 'v-if' directive renders the element if the given expression resolves to true, 'v-else-if' is used for else if condition and 'v-else' is used for else condition.

```
<p v-if="loggedIn">Welcome!</p>
<p v-else-if="loggedOut">Please log in.</p>
<p v-else>Invalid user.</p>
```

4. **v-for**: This directive is used for rendering lists of items.

```
<ul>
  <li v-for="item in items">{{ item }}</li>
</ul>
```

5. **v-model**: It creates two-way data bindings on form 'input', 'textarea', and 'select' elements. It's mostly used with form elements, allowing the form field to update a Vue data property and vice versa.

```
<input v-model="message" placeholder="edit me">
```

6. **v-show**: This directive toggles the visibility of an element, using the CSS 'display' property.

```
<h1 v-show="showTitle">Hello World</h1>
```

7. **v-text & v-html**: The 'v-text' directive updates the 'textContent' of an element whereas 'v-html' directive updates the 'innerHTML' of an element.

```
<span v-text="msg"></span>
<span v-html="rawHtml"></span>
```

8. **v-cloak**: This directive remains on the element until the associated Vue instance finishes compilation. It's often used with CSS rules to hide un-compiled mustache bindings until the Vue instance is compiled.

```
<div v-cloak>{{ message }}</div>
```

9. **v-once**: This directive renders the element and its directives once only. On subsequent re-renders, the element/tag will be treated as static content and skipped.

```
<span v-once>Only rendered once: {{ msg }}</span>
```

10. **v-pre**: This directive skips compilation for this element and all its children elements. It can be used to display raw mustache tags.

```
<span v-pre>{{ rawMessage }}</span>
```

These directives, when used right, can make your Vue.js code cleaner and more understandable. They're one of the things that makes Vue.js easy to pick up and integrate with other libraries or existing projects.

2.12   How do you handle user input, like clicking a button, in Vue?

Vue.js uses a directive called v-on to attach event listeners that invoke methods on Vue instances. When a Vue method is invoked, it has access to special variables like $event so it can access the DOM event in an event handler.

For example, let's say we have a button and we want to handle the user clicking it. First, we create a Vue instance with a method we want to run when the button is clicked:

```
let app = new Vue({
  el: '#app',
```

```
data: {
  message: 'Hello␣Vue!'
},
methods: {
  handleClick: function (event) {
    alert(this.message);
  }
}
});
```

Then, in the HTML, we would use the v-on directive to link the handleClick method to the button's click event:

```
<div id="app">
  <button v-on:click="handleClick">Click Me</button>
</div>
```

When the button is clicked, the handleClick method will be called and Vue will display an alert with the message stored in the data property.

Also, the v-on:click directive can be shortened just to @click for convenience.

```
<button @click="handleClick">Click Me</button>
```

In addition, Vue also allows adding modifiers to the event handling, for specific key events, mouse button events, etc. For example, with v-on:click.prevent, the system will stop the default action for that event to occur.

```
<button @click.prevent="handleClick">Click Me</button>
```

In this case, the .prevent is event modifiers. They are used to indicate that some default behavior should happen when the event is triggered.

2.13   What is a computed property? How is it different from a method?

A computed property in Vue.js is a simple JavaScript function that is used as a property in an object. It is mainly used for asynchronous or expensive operations, where you wish to limit the rate of execution.

Technically, computed properties in Vue.js are more of reactive dependencies, where a computed property will only re-evaluate if some of its reactive dependencies have changed. This is in contrast to methods, which will always re-run whenever a re-render occurs. As a result, computed properties significantly improve the performance when dealing with complex logic that depends on reactive data.

Here's the basic syntax for a computed property:

```
var vm = new Vue({
  el: '#example',
  data: {
    message: 'Hello'
  },
  computed: {
    // a computed getter
    reversedMessage: function () {
      // `this` points to the vm instance
      return this.message.split('').reverse().join('')
    }
  }
})
```

And here's a method doing the same thing:

```
var vm = new Vue({
  el: '#example',
  data: {
    message: 'Hello'
  },
  methods: {
    reversedMessage: function () {
      // `this` points to the vm instance
      return this.message.split('').reverse().join('')
    }
  }
})
```

Although both examples produce the same output, the main difference is that a computed property will cache the result, only updating it if its dependencies change (i.e., 'message' in the example). This makes computed properties much more efficient when the result is expensive to calculate and the dependencies change infrequently. In contrast, a method will recalculate the result every time it's invoked, regardless of whether its dependencies have changed or not. This makes methods more suited to tasks where the result should always be recalculated, regardless of dependencies, such as responding to user input.

In addition, computed properties can also have setters whereas methods cannot:

```
var vm = new Vue({
  el: '#example',
  data: {
    firstName: 'Foo',
    lastName: 'Bar'
  },
  computed: {
    fullName: {
      // getter
      get: function () {
        return this.firstName + '␣' + this.lastName
      },
      // setter
      set: function (newValue) {
        var names = newValue.split('␣')
        this.firstName = names[0]
        this.lastName = names[names.length - 1]
      }
    }
  }
})
```

In this code, 'fullName' is a computed property with both a getter and a setter. The getter will combine 'firstName' and 'lastName', while the setter will split a given name into its components when assigned a new value. This functionality is not available for methods.

2.14   How do you watch for data changes in Vue?

In Vue.js, you can keep track of changes in the data by using the 'watch' property. It is used to observe and react to data changes on a Vue instance.

Below is a simple structure of a 'watch' property with Vue instance:

```
new Vue({
   data: {
       firstName: 'John',
       lastName: 'Doe'
   },
   watch: {
     firstName: function (val) {
       console.log('First name changed to: ', val)
     },
     lastName: function (val) {
       console.log('Last name changed to: ', val)
     }
   }
})
```

Here, the 'watch' property is an object where you define the data properties to watch for changes. When the 'firstName' or 'lastName' changes, Vue calls the corresponding function with the new value ('val').

Also, you can watch for changes in a computed property or in an expression:

```
new Vue({
   data: {
       firstName: 'John',
       lastName: 'Doe'
   },
   computed: {
     fullName: function () {
       return this.firstName + ' ' + this.lastName;
     }
   },
   watch: {
     fullName: function (newVal, oldVal) {
       console.log('Full name changed from: ', oldVal, ' to: ', newVal)
     }
   }
})
```

In the above example, whenever 'fullName' changes, its corresponding function in 'watch' is called with new and old values. This feature is useful whenever an operation needs to be performed upon data change.

Vue offers an elegant way to track data changes and react to them accordingly, which ensures efficient and optimal re-rendering of the component whenever its state changes.

2.15   What is the virtual DOM and how does Vue utilize it?

The Virtual DOM (V-DOM) is a concept in web development that involves creating a light-weight, offline copy of the actual DOM present on the webpage. It is a programming concept where an ideal or "virtual" representation of a UI is kept in memory and synced with the "real" DOM by a library such as React (or Vue) through a process called diffing.

Vue creates a lighter version of an actual DOM, retains it, and uses it to watch for changes. It does this using its "reactivity system". When a user interacts with the webpage (like clicking a button), instead of making changes to the actual DOM, Vue updates the virtual DOM. It then compares (diffs) the virtual DOM with the actual DOM, identifies the differences (the "diffs"), and applies these diffs to the real DOM.

This technique provides a couple of advantages:

1. **Performance**: Making changes to the actual DOM is expensive. With the virtual DOM, Vue makes minimal changes, resulting in highly efficient and faster updates to the real DOM.

2. **Efficiency**: The diffing algorithm only modifies elements that have actually changed in the DOM rather than having to recreate entire DOM nodes, leading to optimized performance and less memory

consumption.

For example, if we have the following Vue template:

```
<template>
  <div>
    <p>{{ message }}</p>
  </div>
</template>

<script>
export default {
  data() {
    return {
      message: 'Hello, Vue!'
    }
  }
}
</script>
```

In the template above, Vue creates a render function which returns
a virtual DOM node tree. If the 'message' changes, Vue identifies
this change, generates a new V-DOM tree, and efficiently updates
the real DOM to match the changes. This simplifies the process
and ensures that the most minimal work is done for each change,
improving performance.

2.16   How do you include external libraries or plugins in a Vue project?

To include external libraries or plugins in a Vue.js project, you have
a few different options.

1. Using '<script>' or '<link>' tags in 'index.html'

This is the most direct and simplest method. You just have to add
'<script>' or '<link>' tags to the HTML file.

```
<script src="https://cdnjs.cloudflare.com/ajax/libs/jquery/3.3.1/jquery.min.
    js"></script>
```

However, this method is not recommended for large applications because it's not modular and cannot take advantage of webpack's optimization features.

2. Importing in main.js

In your main.js file (or whichever file is the entry point for your application), you can import libraries or plugins using the import statement. For example, to use lodash:

```
import _ from 'lodash';
```

Once you've imported lodash here, you can use it anywhere in your vue application.

3. Importing in individual components

You can also import libraries or plugins in individual Vue.js components as needed also using the import command.

```
// In your component
import _ from 'lodash';

export default {
  name: 'example-component',
  methods: {
    someMethod() {
      _.isEmpty(this.someData) // use lodash inside this method
    }
  }
}
```

4. Using Vue.use()

To use Vue plugins, vue-router, vuex, etc, it is recommended to use 'Vue.use()' which installs a Vue.js plugin. Once installed, this plugin can add global mixins, add instance methods, etc. to Vue.js

```
//main.js
import Vue from 'vue'
import Vuex from 'vuex'
Vue.use(Vuex)
```

This allows the plugin to augment the Vue core in a decoupled way.

5. NPM or Yarn

For libraries available as packages, you can use a package manager
like npm or yarn to install them. Then, you can import them in your
file as explained before.

```
# using npm
npm install lodash

# using yarn
yarn add lodash
```

Please remember to always keep in mind the dependencies and loads
of the libraries you are integrating. Avoid adding unused or unnecessary external libraries into your Vue project, as this can significantly
affect your project's performance.

2.17   How do you handle form input in Vue?

In Vue.js, handling form input can be done using the 'v-model' directive. This creates a two-way binding between the form input and the
application data.

Here's an example of how to handle form input in Vue:

```
<div id="app">
  <input v-model="message" placeholder="edit me">
  <p>Message is: {{ message }}</p>
</div>

new Vue({
  el: '#app',
  data: {
    message: ''
  }
})
```

In this code, an input field is created, and the 'v-model' directive is
used to bind its value to a data property ('message' in this case).
This property gets updated every time the content of the input field
changes, and at the same time any changes to this property in your
Vue instance will also update the content of the input field.

When handling form input, it's important to note the following:

1. By default, 'v-model' synchronizes the input with the data after each 'input' event, which occurs after every key press. However, you can add a lazy modifier, like 'v-model.lazy', to instead sync after change events, which usually occur after the input is blurred.

2. If the initial value of your expression inside 'v-model' is null, '<input>' will treat it as the string "null" as a default value. Hence, you should typically initialize your data to a string.

3. When used together with a 'v-for', you have to provide a unique 'key' attribute for each item.

4. Checkboxes and radio buttons require an extra layer of handling. For multiple checkboxes bound to the same array, you need to use the same 'v-model' with them. For radio buttons, bind each to the same variable.

Example for handling checkboxes:

```
<div id="app">
  <input type="checkbox" id="jack" value="Jack" v-model="checkedNames">
  <label for="jack">Jack</label>
  <input type="checkbox" id="john" value="John" v-model="checkedNames">
  <label for="john">John</label>
  <input type="checkbox" id="mike" value="Mike" v-model="checkedNames">
  <label for="mike">Mike</label>
  <p>Checked names: {{ checkedNames }}</p>
</div>
```

```
new Vue({
  el: '#app',
  data: {
    checkedNames: []
  }
})
```

In this example, the 'checkedNames' array is bound to the value of the checked checkboxes. When a checkbox is checked or unchecked, the corresponding value is added or removed from the array.

2.18   What is Vue CLI? Why is it useful?

Vue CLI, or Vue Command Line Interface, is a full system for rapid Vue.js development. It provides a standard build setup for applications that aim at being flexible and powerful. It was launched to quickly scaffold single-page applications. With Vue CLI, setting up a new project is quick and easy, saving developers the routine configurations and setups.

There are several reasons why Vue CLI is particularly useful:

1. **Scaffolding**: Vue CLI helps in generating a new project or parts of a project. This is very useful in the initial stages of project development for building the basic directory and file structure.

2. **Simplifying Build Processes**: Vue CLI comes prepackaged with a build tool either webpack or rollup. This makes it easier to start writing code without having to worry about setting up a development environment and build process.

3. **Inbuilt Server with Livereload**: Vue CLI comes with an inbuilt server that can be activated with the command "vue serve". This server also supports hot-reloads, which means it reflects the changes made in the code on the browser without a manual restart.

4. **Configurable**: Vue CLI is entirely configurable without ejecting, which means you can edit the internal configuration without the dreaded "eject" command.

5. **Plugin system**: Vue CLI has a rich set of official plugins that can be added to the project at any time. This big ecosystem around Vue CLI provides developers with many pre-configured solutions.

Here is an example of how you create a project using Vue CLI:

```
# Install Vue CLI globally if it's not already installed
npm install -g @vue/cli

# Create a new project
vue create my-project-name
```

In this command, "'my-project-name'" should be replaced with the desired name of your project. After running the "'vue create'" command, it will prompt you to pick a preset. You can either choose the default preset which comes with a basic Babel + ESLint setup or manually select features for a more tailor-made setup. This shows the flexibility of using Vue CLI for your project.

2.19   How do you manage state in a Vue application?

Managing the state in a Vue.js application can be done in several ways, each suitable for different use cases. Let's start by explaining what we mean by 'state'. In Vue.js, the state of an application refers to the data and the variables that can change throughout the life cycle of the application.

1. **Local State:** The most basic way of managing state in Vue is to use local state within Vue components. Every Vue component has its own local state that can be defined in its 'data' property. The 'data' function returns an object containing the initial data for the component. This data can then be accessed and manipulated throughout the component.

```
const MyApp = new Vue({
  data: {
    message: 'Hello␣Vue!'
  }
});
```

2. **Props and Events:** For parent-child communication, Vue uses a combination of props and events. Props allow parent components to pass data down to child components. Events allow child components to communicate with their parents by emitting custom events to which the parent can listen.

```
// Child Component
Vue.component('my-component', {
  props: ['myProp'],
```

```
    template: '<div>{{ myProp }}</div>'
});

// Parent Component
<my-component v-bind:myProp="parentData"></my-component>
```

3. **Vuex:** For more complex applications, where multiple components might share and mutate the same data, or where the data flow
doesn't fit a parent-child relationship, Vue provides Vuex. Vuex is a
state management library that follows the Flux architecture, and is
directly inspired by Redux. Vuex is integrated into Vue's devtools extension, which makes it easier to track when and where state changes
happened.

With Vuex, the state of the application is kept in a centralized store,
that can be mutated by actions and mutations. Components can then
map state to local computed properties, or dispatch actions.

Here is a simple Vuex store:

```
const store = new Vuex.Store({
  state: {
    count: 0
  },
  mutations: {
    increment (state) {
      state.count++
    }
  }
})
```

In summary, Vue provides several ways of managing state, each suitable for different scenarios. For small-scale applications, local state
might be enough. For medium-scale applications, using props and
events might be the best fit. For larger applications with complex
data flow and components interaction, Vuex is likely the best option.

2.20 What is the difference between local and global registration of a Vue component?

Registration of a Vue component can be done in two ways - Local Registration and Global Registration.

1. Local Registration: In local registration, the component is only available within the component where it is registered. If you're only using the component in one place, or the component is a child-only component, then local registration is appropriate. It's a good idea to locally register a component whenever possible because it encapsulates the component to just the parts of the app that need it.

Example of local registration:

```
const ComponentA = { /* ... */ }

export default {
  components: {
    ComponentA
  },
  // ...
}
```

2. Global Registration: In global registration, the component is available throughout the application. If the component is being used in multiple places, it makes sense to declare it globally. However, globally registered "base" components can be auto-imported in webpack so they're always available. No import required.

Example of global registration:

```
Vue.component('component-a', { /* ... */ })
Vue.component('component-b', { /* ... */ })
```

So, the major difference between local and global registration of Vue component is their scope of availability within the application. Global registration makes a component available throughout your app, while local registration restricts it to the part of the app where it is declared.

This is an important aspect in terms of app performance and optimization. And thus, the choice between local and global registration depends on specific use case and project needs.

Chapter 3

Intermediate

3.1 Explain the difference between props and data in a Vue component.

In Vue.js, both props and data are used to pass information. However, they play distinct roles and are utilized in different contexts:

1. 'Props': Props, short for properties, are used to pass data from parent components down to their child components. It's a way of customizing the child component, supplying it with data that it can use in its own template and methods. This allows child components to reuse logic already implemented in parent components, leading to more manageable and maintainable code. It's important to mention that props in Vue are always one-way data flow, meaning that if you change the prop value in a child component it WON'T affect the parent component's original value.

Here's a simple use of props:

```
// Parent component
<template>
```

```
<div>
  <child-component :myProp="parentData"/>
</div>
</template>

<script>
import ChildComponent from './ChildComponent.vue'

export default {
  data() {
    return {
      parentData: 'Hello␣World'
    }
  },
  components: {
    ChildComponent
  }
}
</script>
```

In ChildComponent.vue:

```
// Child component
<template>
  <div>
    {{ myProp }}
  </div>
</template>

<script>
export default {
  props: ['myProp']
}
</script>
```

2. 'Data': The 'data' option in Vue components is used to declare local state. Each instance/component maintains its isolated copy of the data object it returns, and changes to its properties do not affect others. Unlike props, changes to data are confined to the component that owns them and will not affect parent components or get propagated to children.

```
<template>
  <div>{{ text }}</div>
</template>

<script>
export default {
  data() {
    return {
      text: 'Hello␣Vue!'
    }
  }
}
```

```
</script>
```

In this example, 'text' is a local data property for the component and can be changed from within the component, but these changes will not affect any parent or child components.

In summary, the key differences between props and data are:

- 'Props' serve as the inputs for components and allow parent components to pass data down to child components.

- 'Data' is owned and managed by the component itself – it represents the internal state of the component.

- 'Props' are passed down from the parent and are immutable within the child component, while data properties can be changed within its owner component.

3.2 How do you handle parent-child communication beyond props?

In Vue.js, communication between parent and child components is typically done using props. However, beyond props, there are several different ways to handle parent-child communication:

1. **Event Emitting**: The child component can emit an event, and the parent can listen to that event. The '$emit' instance method is used to trigger events in the child component, and the 'v-on' directive or "@event" is used to listen to events in the parent component.

```
// Child Component
this.$emit('child-event', eventData);

// Parent Component
<child-component @child-event="parentMethod"></child-component>
```

2. **Using Vuex for State Management**: Vuex is a state management library for Vue.js. It serves as a centralized store for all the components in an application, with rules ensuring that the state can

only be mutated in a predictable fashion. It integrates well with the official devtools extension, providing advanced features such as zero-config time-travel debugging and state snapshot import / export.

3. **'provide'/'inject' method**: This is another method you can use to communicate between ancestor and descendant components, regardless of how deep they are nested or whether they have a direct parent-child relationship. The parent component has a 'provide' option to provide data, and the descendant components use the 'inject' option to start using this provided data.

Note: it's worth mentioning that the 'provide/inject' bindings are NOT reactive, unless a reactive object is provided.

These methods give you several different ways to handle communication between parent and child components. The right method to use depends on the specific requirements of your application.

3.3   What are mixins in Vue? Provide an example use case.

Mixins in Vue.js are a flexible way to distribute reusable functionalities for Vue components. A mixin object can contain any component option. When a component uses a mixin, all options in the mixin will be "mixed" into the component's own options.

Mixins can contain various Vue component properties like data, methods, computed properties, lifecycle hooks, directives, and so on. When you use a mixin, all these configurations are merged into your Vue component.

For example, you may have some helper methods that you use across components. Instead of repeating these methods in each component, you can create and include a mixin. Let's illustrate this:

```
// Defining a mixin
let myMixin = {
```

```
  created: function () {
    this.hello()
  },
  methods: {
    hello: function () {
      console.log('Hello from the mixin!')
    }
  }
}

// Defining a component
let Component = Vue.extend({
  mixins: [myMixin]
})

let component = new Component() // => "Hello from the mixin!"
```

In this example, the 'Component' instance invokes the 'hello' method when created. That method itself is declared in the mixin.

However, when we use mixins, we should also be aware of the potential for conflicts, as methods, computed properties, and hooks will be merged into the component's options. The component's options will take precedence if a conflict arises. Also, when hooks from mixins and the component itself coincide, they are both triggered without overriding each other, and the mixin's hook is triggered first.

3.4   How do you handle custom events in Vue?

Custom events in Vue.js are used to handle interaction between child and parent components. With Vue.js, child components can trigger events that parent components can listen to and react accordingly. This is how the flow of data is managed from child to parent.

To handle custom events in Vue, you have three key steps:

1. In the child component, emit an event using the 'this.$emit' function.

2. In the parent component, listen for the event.

3. When the event is caught in the parent component, execute a function.

Here is a detailed example:

Let us imagine we have a user component ('User.vue') and want to notify the parent component every time the name of that User changes.

First, in the 'User.vue' component:

```
<template>
  <div>
    <input v-model="username" @input="notifyParent">
  </div>
</template>

<script>
export default {
  data() {
    return {
      username: ''
    }
  },
  methods: {
    notifyParent() {
      this.$emit('username-changed', this.username)
    }
  }
}
</script>
```

In the code above, we're emitting a 'username-changed' event whenever the username changes, passing 'this.username' as the payload of the event.

Then, in the parent component:

```
<template>
  <user @username-changed="handleUsernameChanged"></user>
</template>

<script>
import User from './User.vue'
export default {
  components: {
    User
  },
  methods: {
    handleUsernameChanged(newUsername) {
      // handle the new username here
    }
  }
}
</script>
```

The parent component is listening for the 'username-changed' event, and calls 'handleUsernameChanged' when that event is caught. The new username is passed as an argument to that function.

That's how you handle custom events in Vue.js. They are particularly useful for handling state changes that need to communicated from child components to parent components.

3.5 Explain the concept of single-file components in Vue.

Single-file components in Vue.js are a paradigm that allows you to define your component structure in a highly modular way. It's called single-file components because you define the entirety of a component, including its functionality, template, and styles, in a single file.

A single-file Vue component has a .vue extension and consists of three parts:

1. '<template>': This is where the HTML template of the component is defined. This is the visible part of the component and can include other components, directives, or data from the Vue instance.

2. '<script>': This is where the JavaScript code for the component is defined. This includes the Vue instance, component data, methods, computed properties, lifecycle hooks, etc.

3. '<style>': This is where the CSS styles for the component are defined. Styles can be scoped to the component or can be global.

Here's an example of what a single-file component might look like:

```
<template>
  <div class="my-component">
    <h1>{{ message }}</h1>
  </div>
</template>

<script>
```

```
export default {
    data() {
        return {
            message: 'Hello,␣Vue!'
        }
    }
}
</script>

<style scoped>
.my-component {
    font-size: 2em;
    color: #42b983;
}
</style>
```

In this example, "message" is a piece of data that is rendered in the template. The style is scoped, meaning it will only apply to elements in this component's template.

One of the biggest advantages of single-file components is that they allow for a high degree of modularity. Since everything related to the component is defined in one place, it's easy to understand and manage the component's design and functionality. Plus, single-file components can be imported and used in other components, making code reuse simple and straightforward.

However, to use single-file components, you need to use a build tool like Webpack or Browserify to bundle your components into a single file that the browser can understand. Vue CLI can set up this build process for you.

3.6   How do you handle transitions and animations in Vue?

Transitions and animations in Vue.js are handled using the built-in '<transition>' and '<transition-group>' components.

Here is a basic example:

```
<transition name="fade">
  <div v-if="show">Hello</div>
```

```
</transition>
```

In this case, the 'v-if' directive toggles the presence of the element in the DOM. The "fade" transition effect is automatically applied whenever the element is inserted or removed.

Under the hood, Vue automatically adds/removes CSS classes at appropriate times to trigger CSS transitions or animations. For the "fade" transition effect, Vue will apply these classes:

- 'fade-enter': Added at the start of the entering transition. Removed after one frame.

- 'fade-enter-active': Added during the entire entering transition. Removed when the transition finishes.

- 'fade-enter-to': Added one frame after the start of the enter transition (at the same time 'fade-enter' is removed), removed when the transition finishes.

- 'fade-leave': Added at the start of the leaving transition. Removed after one frame.

- 'fade-leave-active': Added during the entire leaving transition. Removed when the transition finishes.

- 'fade-leave-to': Added one frame after the start of the leave transition (at the same time 'fade-leave' is removed), removed when the transition finishes.

And the corresponding CSS for the fade transition would be:

```
.fade-enter-active, .fade-leave-active {
  transition: opacity .5s;
}
.fade-enter, .fade-leave-to {
  opacity: 0;
}
```

This will fade elements in and out as they enter and leave the DOM.

If you need more control over the transition durations or timing function, you can use a JavaScript hook in your component:

```
<transition
```

```
@before-enter="beforeEnter"
@enter="enter"
@after-enter="afterEnter"
@enter-cancelled="enterCancelled"
@before-leave="beforeLeave"
@leave="leave"
@after-leave="afterLeave"
@leave-cancelled="leaveCancelled"
  >
```

In these hooks, you can use JavaScript or Vue's animation system to create more complex transitions or animations.

For list transitions, Vue.js provides the '<transition-group>' component. It renders a 'span' by default, but you can change its element and transition system to fit your needs.

3.7   What is the difference between v-show and v-if?

The 'v-if' and 'v-show' are both conditional rendering directives in Vue.js, but they work in a slightly different way.

'v-if' is "real" conditional rendering because it ensures that event listeners and child components inside the conditional block are properly destroyed and re-created during toggles.

'v-if' is also lazy: if the condition is false on initial render, it will not do anything - the conditional block won't be rendered until the condition becomes true.

In other words, 'v-if' works by actually adding or removing elements from the DOM, which can be an expensive operation in terms of performance. This means that if you're frequently toggling something on/off, 'v-if' could be slower because it has to recreate the element each time.

Here's a simple example with v-if:

```
<div v-if="show">This will be either added to or removed from the DOM</div>
```

On the other hand, 'v-show' simply toggles the CSS display property of the element. It doesn't care about the initial condition, the element is always rendered regardless of the initial condition.

This means that 'v-show' is much simpler and faster for elements that are switched on and off a lot, but slower for the initial render if the element is supposed to be hidden, because it always renders its content.

Here's a simple example with v-show:

```
<div v-show="show">The CSS display property of this will be toggled</div>
```

So to summarize, 'v-if' has a real structural impact on the DOM (i.e., it adds or removes elements), and should be used when the condition is unlikely to change at runtime. 'v-show' doesn't change the structure of the DOM, just the visibility of elements, therefore it is better if the condition changes very often at runtime.

3.8   How do you make API calls in a Vue application?

API calls in a Vue.js application can be made by utilizing the popular HTTP clients such as 'Axios', 'Vue-Resource' or the browser's built-in 'Fetch API'. However, the Vue team recommends using Axios.

In order to make an API request using Axios:

1. First, you need to install it. It can be installed via npm/yarn or by linking via a CDN as follows:

- npm/yarn:

```
npm install axios
# OR
```

```
yarn add axios
```

- CDN:

```
<script src="https://unpkg.com/axios/dist/axios.min.js"></script>
```

2. After installation, you can import axios into your '.vue' component
and use it to make HTTP requests like so:

```
<script>
import axios from 'axios';

export default {
  name: 'Sample.vue',
  data() {
    return {
      posts: null
    }
  },
  created() {
    axios
      .get('https://jsonplaceholder.typicode.com/posts')
      .then(response => (this.posts = response.data))
      .catch(error => console.log(error))
  },
}
</script>
```

In the API request made above, the '.get' method is used to make a
'GET' request to retrieve data from the specified URL—
'https://jsonplaceholder.typicode.com/posts'.

The '.then' method is chained to handle the response from the server
when the request is successful. In the callback function provided to
the '.then' method, response.data is assigned to this.posts, allowing
you to display the retrieved data in your Vue component.

The '.catch' method is used to handle any errors that may occur
when making the HTTP request. In the callback function supplied to
this method, the error object is logged to the console for debugging
purposes.

In real-world applications, it's a best practice to handle API calls
from Vuex actions to manage state efficiently. Moreover, server-side
exceptions and errors should be handled properly. You can also inte-

grate Axios instance with Vue instance using vue-axios which provides more Vue-like style to make HTTP requests.

3.9 Describe component slots and their use cases.

In Vue.js, slots are a powerful feature that allow you to compose components in a flexible way. They are a mechanism for Vue components that allows you to compose your components in a variety of ways.

Slots give you the ability to insert your own template logic into space that is carved out in a child component. Specifically, they allow you to define a place in your component's template which can be filled with any code you want, which is particularly useful when you want to make the component more reusable and flexible for whatever context it's used in.

There are two types of slots: unnamed slots & named slots.

1. **Unnamed Slots**: These are the basic version of slots. Anything not surrounded by a '<slot>' tag in the template of a child component is considered as the content for unnamed slot. Here's an example:

Child Component:

```
<template>
  <div>
    <slot></slot>
  </div>
</template>
```

Parent Component:

```
<template>
  <child-component>
    <h1>Hello, World!</h1>
  </child-component>
</template>
```

In this example, the '<h1>' tag in the parent component will replace the '<slot>' tag in the child component.

2. **Named Slots**: These are more specific and allow you to provide several different slots in your child component. In your child component, you can have different '<slot>' tags with different "name" attributes, and then in the parent you can insert different content for each slot. Here's an example:

Child Component:

```
<template>
  <div>
    <header>
      <slot name="header"></slot>
    </header>
    <main>
      <slot></slot>
    </main>
    <footer>
      <slot name="footer"></slot>
    </footer>
  </div>
</template>
```

Parent Component:

```
<child-component>
  <template #header>
    <h1>Hello, World!</h1>
  </template>
  <p>This is some main content.</p>
  <template #footer>
    <button>Click me!</button>
  </template>
</child-component>
```

In this case, the specific template fits into the specific named slots in the child component.

Use Cases: - **Dialog/Modal Components**: Slots can be very useful in a dialog or a modal component, where you have some common wrapper markup (including some JavaScript behavior), but you want to customize the title, the main content, and the set of buttons available.

 - **Layout Components**: Slots can be handy when you have a common layout structure and want to change the content.

- **Reusable controls/inputs**: You can build a flexible Input component where label, validation messages, and input control can be handled by slots.

3.10 How do you handle form validation in Vue?

Form validation in Vue.js can be handled in several ways. Among these are two main strategies: manual validation and using a Vue.js library specifically designed for form validation.

1. Manual Validation: This approach involves binding the form values to data properties in the Vue.js instance and using computed properties or watchers to check these values for validity.

Here is a simple example of manual form validation for a text input field:

```
new Vue({
    el: '#app',
    data: {
        name: ''
    },
    computed: {
        nameIsValid() {
            return this.name.length > 0;
        }
    }
});
```

In this case, the 'nameIsValid' computed property will be 'true' if the name is not an empty string, and 'false' otherwise. This can be used in the template to conditionally display error messages.

2. Using a Vue.js Validation Library: There are several libraries available that provide additional functionality and make form validation easier and more sophisticated.

One such library is Vuelidate, which provides a lot of powerful features including model-based validation and asynchronous validation. Here is similar validation with Vuelidate:

```
import { required } from 'vuelidate/lib/validators'

new Vue({
    el: '#app',
    data: {
        name: ''
    },
    validations: {
        name: {
            required
        }
    }
});
```

In this case, the 'required' validation from Vuelidate will check that the name is not an empty string.

Another popular library for form validation in Vue.js is VeeValidate. It offers a wider range of functions like different rules for validation, error message customization, and integration with different CSS frameworks.

Regardless of the approach you choose, the result of the validation (i.e., whether the form fields are valid or not) is typically used in the Vue.js template to conditionally display error messages to the user, and to disable or enable the form's submit button.

3.11   Explain the Vue reactivity system. How does it track changes to data?

Vue.js uses a reactive data system. When you pass a plain JavaScript object to a Vue instance as its data option, Vue wraps each property with a getter/setter using Object.defineProperty. This is an ES5-only and un-shimmable feature, which is why Vue doesn't support IE8 and below.

Here's a simplified illustration of how it works:

```
var data = { a: 1 }
var vm = new Vue({
  data: data
})
vm.a == data.a // => true
```

When you change the value of 'a', the view will automatically re-render with the new updated value.

```
vm.a = 2 // the data property 'a' gets changed
data.a // -> 2; reflected in the original data object
```

The same is true for the opposite:

```
data.a = 3
vm.a // -> 3; Vue instance property gets updated
```

These reactive connections are tracked and formed during the instance initialization phase, in the 'data' property part of the option. Only the object properties that exist when the instance has been created are reactive:

```
vm.b = 2
// `b` is NOT reactive as it was not part of the initial data object
```

Beyond just tracking changes, another key aspect of the reactivity system is its dependence tracking and change propagation - collectors (or watchers) subscribe themselves to observables, and observables notify them when changes occur.

A key advantage of this reactivity system is that it allows Vue to smartly figure out which components exactly need to be re-rendered whenever data changes, without requiring the developer to manually track and declare all data dependencies. This leads to significant performance gains and lesser code complexity.

For tracking arrays, Vue cannot detect mutation when you directly set an item with the index, e.g. 'vm.items[indexOfItem] = newValue' or when you modify the length of the array. For such cases, Vue provides special methods, like 'set'and'splice'.

To allow Vue to track the changing state of objects that wouldn't

otherwise be reactive, Vue provides a '$set' method as well. It allows
you to add a new property to an object and ensure it becomes reactive.

```
this.$set(this.someObject, 'b', 2)

// or using Vue.set globally
Vue.set(this.someObject, 'b', 2)
```

$set also works with arrays, and can be a handy way to overcome the
array change-detection caveat.

The above samples provide a brief insight into Vue's reactivity system.
For more complex scenarios, Vue provides computed properties and
methods to respond to data changes, giving developers a powerful
way to express how data should be transformed and manipulated
over time.

3.12   What are filters in Vue and how are they used?

Filters in Vue.js are a functionality that allow you to apply common
text formatting. They're simple JavaScript functions that take in a
value (the input) and return another value (the output). They are
often used for formatting text in view templates.

The syntax for using a filter in Vue is the pipe symbol (|) followed by
the name of the filter you want to apply. This is similar to how filters
work in Angular or Unix commands.

Here is the basic syntax using Vue's interpolation with curly braces '
':

```
{{ message | filterName }}
```

If the 'filterName' function is defined, the value of 'message' will be
passed into 'filterName' as its first argument.

Filters can be defined locally or globally.

A global filter might look like this:

```
Vue.filter('filterName', function(value) {
    // transform value
});
```

In contrast, a local filter for a Vue component might be defined like this:

```
new Vue({
  filters: {
    filterName: function(value) {
      // transform value
    }
  }
})
```

You can chain filters using the pipe symbol. This example applies 'filterA' and then 'filterB' to 'message':

```
{{ message | filterA | filterB }}
```

Let's say you want to create a filter that capitalizes every word in a string. Here's what it might look like:

```
Vue.filter('capitalize', function(value) {
  if (!value) return ''
  value = value.toString()
  return value.replace(/bw/g, function(letter) {
    return letter.toUpperCase();
  })
})
```

Then use it in a template like this:

```
<div>{{ 'hello␣world' | capitalize }}</div>
```

The output would be: "Hello World".

It's important to note that Vue.js filters don't change the original data, they only change the output and return a filtered version of it.

While they can be very useful for small formatting tasks within templates, the official Vue.js guide encourages developers to use computed properties, methods, or watchers for more complex logic.

3.13   How do you use local state in a Vue component?

In Vue.js, a component's local state is defined in the 'data' function. This is where you initialize all the variables that you want to be reactive. The properties in the data object works very similar to the properties in the Vue instance, i.e., they get reactive and also get added to Vue's reactivity system.

Here's an example:

```
Vue.component('my-component', {
  // define the data function
  data: function() {
    // return the initial data object
    return {
      count: 0,
      message: 'Hello␣Vue!'
    };
  },
  // use the local state in a method
  methods: {
    incrementCount() {
      this.count++;
    }
  }
});
```

In this sample Vue component, 'count' and 'message' are part of the local component's state. These are reactive, meaning that Vue.js will update the DOM automatically if their values change.

For example, imagine you have a button in your component's template that calls the 'incrementCount' method when it's clicked:

```
<template>
  <div>
    <p>{{ count }}</p>
    <p>{{ message }}</p>
    <button @click="incrementCount">Increment</button>
  </div>
</template>
```

Whenever this button is clicked, the count will increase and the updated count will be displayed, thanks to Vue's reactive nature. Note that these data properties are only accessible in the scope of this component and are not shared between other components. However, the values can be passed to child components using props, or using a centralized store like Vuex in case of a large scale application where state needs to be shared across multiple components.

The 'data' must be a function that returns an object, since each instance should have an isolated scope i.e., having its own local state so that changing data in one component does not affect data in other instances of the same component.

3.14   Describe the use of nextTick in Vue.

The Vue 'nextTick' function is used for delaying the execution of a piece of code until the next DOM update cycle. This can be useful in cases where you want to wait for Vue.js to finish updating the DOM before executing a certain piece of code.

Vue.js asynchronously executes DOM updates. This happens when you change some of your data and Vue.js calculates whether the DOM needs to be updated. This is done in a different task and doesn't block the UI while these computations take place. However, sometimes you might want to access or manipulate the DOM directly after these updates. If you try to access the DOM just after changing the data, you might get inconsistent or unexpected results because the DOM might not have been updated yet.

This is where 'nextTick' comes in handy. When called, the 'nextTick' function will delay the execution of your code until Vue.js has finished updating the DOM.

Here is an example:

```
new Vue({
  el: '#app',
  data: {
    message: 'Hello Vue.js!'
  },
  methods: {
```

```
    changeMessage: function() {
      this.message = 'Hello␣nextTick!'
      this.$nextTick(function() {
        console.log(document.querySelector('#app').innerText)
        // output: "Hello nextTick!"
      })
    }
  }
})
```

In the 'changeMessage' method, we are changing the 'message' data
and then using 'nextTick' to log the content of '#app'. Without
'nextTick', the console.log might still print the old 'message', 'Hello
Vue.js!', because Vue.js might not have completed the DOM update
when the log function is executed.

3.15   How do you handle global state management in Vue without using Vuex?

While Vuex is a common method for handling global state management in Vue.js because of its built-in patterns, there are also other
ways to handle global state without using Vuex.

A. Vue Observable:

From Vue 2.6.0, Vue.js provides a built-in method based on Observables for state management. Every Vue component essentially becomes an Observer of the observed data. Meaning, any change in
observed data causes Vue components to re-render. Here's how to
use it:

```
const GlobalState = Vue.observable({ counter: 0 })

new Vue({
  el: '#app',
  computed: {
    counter() {
      return GlobalState.counter;
    }
  },
  methods: {
    increment() {
      GlobalState.counter++;
```

```
    }
  }
})
```

In the code above, we created a global state for our counter, and we used Vue.observable() to make it reactive. We then used computed property to read the state, and the method to modify.

B. Event Bus:

An Event Bus is another effective way of handling state management across components. You can create a new Vue instance and use it as a centralized event bus:

```
var bus = new Vue();

// in component A's method
bus.$emit('id-selected', 1);

// in component B's created hook
bus.$on('id-selected', function (id) {
  // ...
})
```

In the above code, component A emits an event that is listened to in component B. Importantly though, an event bus doesn't really manage state - but it can be used in conjunction with other methods to trigger changes or actions.

C. Global Store:

You can create your own simple global store without Vuex, and integrate state, getters, mutations and actions:

```
let store = {
  state: {
    count: 0,
  },
  increment() {
    this.state.count++;
  },
}

new Vue({
  el: '#app',
  data() {
    return {
      store: store
```

```
    }
   }
 })
```

In this example, there is a simple store object with a count state and an increment method. It is added to Vue's data option, which makes it reactive and available within the Vue components.

Please note that these patterns may not be sufficient for larger applications where Vuex would still be recommended due to its capabilities of tracking component dependencies, addition of middleware with plugins, and time-travel debugging capabilities.

3.16   Explain dynamic component rendering in Vue.

Dynamic component rendering in Vue.js is a unique feature that allows you to switch between different components, without losing their respective states, at runtime. Thus, it provides versatility to your application and enhances user experience.

To utilize dynamic component rendering, Vue.js provides a reserved '<component>' element, which is used in conjunction with the 'is' special attribute that specifies which component to load dynamically.

Here is a simple example:

```
<component v-bind:is="currentComponent"></component>
```

In this case, 'currentComponent' is a variable in your data model that should hold the name of the component you want to render. You can change 'currentComponent' at any time, and Vue.js will automatically manage the rendering to match.

Example:

```
data: {
```

```
    currentComponent: 'componentA'
  }
```

If you have three components named 'componentA', 'componentB', and 'componentC' and you want to switch between them, you can simply change the value of 'currentComponent' in your methods or computed properties and Vue.js will immediately render the new component in place of the old one, maintaining the state of each component.

Here is a more complete example:

```
<template>
  <div>
    <button @click="changeComponent('componentA')">Load Component A</button>
    <button @click="changeComponent('componentB')">Load Component B</button>
    <button @click="changeComponent('componentC')">Load Component C</button>

    <component :is="currentComponent"></component>
  </div>
</template>

<script>
import componentA from './componentA.vue';
import componentB from './componentB.vue';
import componentC from './componentC.vue';

export default {
  components: {
    componentA,
    componentB,
    componentC
  },
  data() {
    return {
      currentComponent: 'componentA'
    }
  },
  methods: {
    changeComponent(component) {
      this.currentComponent = component;
    }
  }
}
</script>
```

In this example, clicking on the different buttons will dynamically load different components. The state of each component is preserved whenever it is replaced, so any data or UI changes will be there when the component is re-rendered.

3.17   How do you handle route navigation in Vue using Vue Router?

Vue Router is the official router for Vue.js. It deeply integrates with Vue.js to make building Single Page Applications with Vue.js easier.

Here's a brief outline on how you can integrate route navigation in Vue using Vue Router:

1. **Installation**

First, to use Vue Router in your project, you need to install it using npm or yarn.

```
npm install vue-router
```

or with yarn,

```
yarn add vue-router
```

2. **Import VueRouter**

Once you've installed VueRouter, you need to import it into your application.

```
import Vue from 'vue';
import VueRouter from 'vue-router';
Vue.use(VueRouter);
```

3. **Define Routes**

You can now define routes for your application. A route should be associated with a component. When a user visits a route, the corresponding component is shown.

```
const routes = [
  { path: '/foo', component: Foo },
  { path: '/bar', component: Bar }
];
```

4. **Create the Router Instance**

After defining the routes, the next step is to create the router instance and pass the 'routes' option.

```
const router = new VueRouter({
  routes // short for `routes: routes`
});
```

5. **Mount the Router Instance to the Vue Instance**

You can then mount the router instance to the main Vue instance using the 'router' option.

```
const app = new Vue({
  router
}).$mount('#app');
```

6. **Use router-link for Navigation**

Vue Router provides a '<router-link>' component for navigating around the application.

```
<router-link to="/foo">Go to Foo</router-link>
<router-link to="/bar">Go to Bar</router-link>
```

7. **Display Current Route Content**

The '<router-view>' component is used to render the component of the matched route.

```
<router-view></router-view>
```

With these steps, you can effectively handle route navigation in Vue using Vue Router.

3.18   What are named routes and named views in Vue Router?

In Vue.js, the Vue Router allows for creation of user-friendly routes, which interact with different components in a Vue.js application. Within this system, we have what's known as named routes and named views.

1. Named Routes: Named routes is a feature provided by Vue Router that helps in navigation and redirects. It allows you to assign a name to a particular route. Once this name is assigned, you can use this name whenever you want to redirect or link to that route. This results in cleaner and more manageable code.

Here is an example of how to define a named route,

```
const routes = [
  {
    path: '/user/:userId',
    name: 'user',
    component: User
  }
]
```

In this case, 'user' is the name of the route. Now, you can use this name 'user' to generate a link dynamically as shown below,

```
<router-link :to="{ name: 'user', params: { userId: 123 }}">User</router-link>
```

2. Named Views: In an application, you might want to have multiple views for a specific route. Vue Router provides a feature, named views, that deals with this requirement. It allows you to have multiple <router-view> outlets, each having a unique name.

An example named view configuration looks like this:

```
const routes = [
  {
    path: '/',
    components: {
      default: Home,
      sidebar: Sidebar
```

```
        }
      }
   ]
```

In your Vue components, you can specify different router-views with names that correspond to these defined in your route configuration,

```
<router-view></router-view>
<router-view name="sidebar"></router-view>
```

According to the above route configuration, '/' path will render the 'Home' component in the unnamed <router-view> and 'Sidebar' component in the <router-view> named 'sidebar'.

Both of these features, named routes and named views, greatly enhance the routing flexibility and capacity of Vue.js applications. They let you create more complex UIs while keeping your code maintainable and straightforward.

3.19   How do you handle lazy loading of components in Vue?

Lazy loading is a technique that is primarily used to enhance the performance of a Vue.js application by splitting the application into chunks that can then be loaded on demand or in parallel. This means that as a user navigates your application, the app loads only the components the user needs at any given time, instead of loading all the components at once.

In Vue, we can accomplish lazy loading of components by using 'Vue's async components' and webpack's 'code splitting feature'. In this way, we are quite literally splitting up our compiled JS and loading it on the fly.

Here's an example of an async component:

```
const Foo = () => import('./Foo.vue')
```

This will load the 'Foo.vue' component only when it's needed for rendering, and the webpack will take care of bundling it separately.

In Vue Router, you can use this concept to achieve 'route-level code-splitting'.

```
const router = new VueRouter({
  routes: [
    { path: '/foo', component: () => import('./Foo.vue') }
  ]
})
```

For every route with an async component, a separate chunk is created and lazy-loaded when that particular route is visited. This can dramatically improve the load time performance because you're only loading what's really necessary, and it is very easy to handle with Vue's async components.

Furthermore, Vue also offers the 'vue-loader''s 'lazy-loading feature', where you can group component chunks using "chunk name":

```
const Foo = () => import(/* webpackChunkName: "group-foo" */ './Foo.vue')
const Bar = () => import(/* webpackChunkName: "group-foo" */ './Bar.vue')
const Baz = () => import(/* webpackChunkName: "group-foo" */ './Baz.vue')
```

'Webpack' will group any async module with the same chunk name into the same async chunk. This can be used to group files from the same route (and perhaps even sub-routes) together, resulting in even better performance.

In summary, lazy loading is a great way to optimize a Vue.js app and can be achieved using Vue's async components and webpack's code-splitting and chunking mechanisms.

3.20 Explain the concept of scoped CSS in Vue components.

Scoped CSS in Vue.js is a feature that makes the styles defined within a Vue component exclusive to that component only. This is a powerful tool for structuring your styles in large, complex applications, as it helps to avoid the potential conflict of CSS rules and maintain cleaner stylesheets overall.

In other words, it provides style encapsulation for a component. It limits the CSS of a component to only apply within that component. Therefore, styles defined in one component will not leak out and affect other components.

Here is an example of how to define scoped styles within a Vue component:

```
<template>
  <div id="my-component">
    <!-- Your component's markup goes here -->
  </div>
</template>

<style scoped>
  #my-component {
    background-color: blue;
  }
</style>
```

In the example above, the 'background-color: blue;' style will only ever apply to the '#my-component' div (or any nested elements) within this component specifically. Even if there are other '#my-component' elements elsewhere in your application, the scope of this style is limited to this instance, preventing it from affecting others.

The way Scoped CSS works is by adding data attributes to elements. The Vue-loader, during the build step, adds unique data attributes to component tags and styles. Much like a unique ID, these attributes align with the CSS selectors to make sure styles do not cross boundaries.

For instance, it'll turn above code into something like this:

```
<template>
  <div id="my-component" data-v-3f4abc4>
    <!-- Your component's␣markup␣goes␣here␣-->
␣␣</div>
</template>

<style␣scoped>
␣␣#my-component[data-v-3f4abc4]␣{
␣␣␣␣background-color:␣blue;
␣␣}
</style>
```

While the scoped style approach gives you a high degree of isolation, sometimes you may still need global styles. In such cases, having both scoped and non-scoped styles in your components is perfectly fine.

It's also worth noting that using CSS modules or CSS-in-JS libraries is another viable strategy for style encapsulation in Vue.js, each with its own trade-offs, and the best choice often depends greatly on the specificities of your project and your team's preferences.

Chapter 4

Advanced

4.1 Explain the difference between active and passive event listeners in Vue.

In the context of Vue.js and JavaScript event handling, an event listener can be either active or passive.

1. Active Event Listeners: Active event listeners, also referred to as blocking listeners, are the traditional or default type of event listeners. With an active event listener, the browser will wait for the JavaScript to finish executing before doing anything else like scrolling, typing, etc. During the execution of the JavaScript, you can prevent the default behavior of an event (for instance, prevent scrolling when a user scrolls in a certain div box), by using 'event.preventDefault()'. So, the primary characteristic of an active listener is it's capability to block the default action by calling 'event.preventDefault()'.

In Vue, to create an active event listener, you simply omit the '.passive' modifier in the 'v-on' directive. For example:

```
<div v-on:scroll='scrollHandler'></div>
```

2. Passive Event Listeners: Passive event listeners provide a performance improvement for certain event types, like 'touchstart' and 'touchmove', where you don't want to delay the browser's default handling. Essentially, passive listeners tell the browser that you don't want to prevent any default behavior; the event handling script cannot block other visual updates.

Passive listeners can't cancel the received event because the main thread will page the event even before the execution of the listener function. This can lead to increased smoothness in scrolling and other types of animations.

In Vue, an event listener can be made passive by adding the '.passive' modifier to the 'v-on' directive. For example:

```
<div v-on:scroll.passive='scrollHandler'></div>
```

Important to note that 'event.preventDefault()' won't have any effect inside the event handling function attached to a passive event listener. Trying to call 'preventDefault' inside a passive listener will lead to a console warning.

To summarise, the major difference between the two types lies in the amount of control they provide over the default behaviors associated with certain events. While active event listeners can block the default action and take control, passive listeners let the event handling processes be smoother and quicker by not blocking any default action.

4.2   How does Vue's reactivity system work under the hood? Discuss the role of Object.defineProperty or Proxies.

Vue.js's reactivity system is quite clever and a foundational concept to the framework. Fundamentally, it is a system for tracking changes to data and automatically updating the DOM when data changes.

Vue's reactivity system is primarily built using JavaScript's 'Object.defineProperty()' or Proxies.

How does it work? When you pass a plain JavaScript object to a Vue instance as its 'data' option, Vue walks through each property in the object and converts it using 'Object.defineProperty()' or Proxy (in Vue 3).

In prior versions, Vue used 'Object.defineProperty' to convert passed in data to getters and setters. This property is then observed, or 'made reactive'.

If you modify a reactive property, Vue tracks these changes and updates any part of the application that is using this data.

Here's a crude breakdown of how reactivity is achieved with Object.defineProperty:

1. It recursively traverses the properties of data and converts them into getter/setters for reactivity.

2. In the getter, it collects dependencies - i.e., remembers which parts of the application are using this data.

3. When the setter is triggered on a change, it notifies the dependencies to update their views.

However, 'Object.defineProperty()' has some limitations. It cannot track the addition or deletion of object's property after it's created, and it doesn't support the observation of array-based changes directly (Vue has to include special methods to handle this, like $set).

To overcome these shortcomings, Vue 3.0 replaced 'Object.defineProperty()' with ES6 Proxies.

Here's how reactivity is improved with Proxies:

1. It can trap a total of 13 different operations on target objects. This includes the operations that 'Object.defineProperty()' cannot handle,

allowing it to handle the addition, deletion of properties, and array indexing.

2. Proxies return the target object itself, which allows for direct operations on the object that won't break reactivity.

3. It's much easier to understand and maintain a Proxy-based codebase.

It's also worth noting that Vue uses a "lazy" strategy for dependency-tracking. Actual computations or DOM manipulations are deferred until they're really needed (i.e., when the getter is triggered).

All in all, Vue's reactivity system is key to its efficiency by keeping data consistent across an application and minimizing unneeded rendering.

4.3   Describe the benefits and drawbacks of using Vuex for state management.

Vuex is a state management library developed by the same team as Vue.js. It's intended to make managing state in complex applications simpler and more robust. Vuex provides a centralized data store for all components in an application, with rules ensuring that the state can only be manipulated in a predictable fashion.

Benefits:

1. **Centralized State Management:** Vuex stores the state of your app at one place so that components can share state information instead of passing props down and events up, which can be messy and complicated in complex applications.

2. **Predictability:** Vuex ensures that state changes only occur from mutations which are trackable and predictable. Additionally, each mutation is also trackable by plugins and dev-tools.

3. **Structure and Organization:** Vuex forces you to organize the state of your application in a particular way which makes it scalable and easier to test.

4. **Dev Tools Integration:** Vuex provides debugging tools like history, state snapshot importing exporting, etc., which help developers in application development and issue resolution.

5. **Plugins:** Vuex enables the developer community to write plugins that can interact with the store. DevTools is a plugin itself.

6. **Time Travel Debugging and hot-reloading:** Time-travelling is another impressive feature about Vuex. With this, you can mutate your state and "travel" back in time to previous states, which makes debugging more welcoming.

Drawbacks:

1. **Learning Curve:** Vuex has a steep learning curve, especially for developers who are not familiar with the Flux architecture or Redux.

2. **Verbosity:** When compared to other ways of managing state, Vuex can be a little verbose due to its structure - actions, mutations, states, getters.

3. **Overkill for Small Apps:** Vuex shines with larger applications with complex state. For simpler applications, Vuex can be overkill and leads to unnecessary complexity.

4. **Hard to understand for beginners:** Beginners may find it a bit hard to understand due to the use of various concepts like getters and mutations.

5. **Boilerplate Code:** As Vuex involves a bit of boilerplate code, it may be cumbersome for some developers to set up the data flow.

Example:

If you need to show a user's name at multiple points in your app, you might get it via an API call and store it within a parent component, passing it down to children components via props. But, if one of those children components needs to change the name (after the user updates their name), you'd either need to find a way to pass this change back upstream to the parent or make another API call for the updated name. Vuex helps deal with this. Every component that needs the username gets it directly from the Vuex store. If one component updates that name, every other component gets the new value immediately.

4.4   How do you handle module organization in Vuex?

Vuex allows for module organization through module namespacing. This feature enables you to divide your store into modules. Each module can contain its own state, mutations, actions, getters, and even nested modules.

The basic structure of a Vuex store looks like this:

```
const store = new Vuex.Store({
  state: {},
  mutations: {},
  actions: {},
  getters: {},
  modules: {
    moduleA: {
      state: () => ({ ... }),
      mutations: { ... },
      actions: { ... },
      getters: { ... },
      modules: {
        subModuleA: {
          state: () => ({ ... }),
          mutations: { ... },
          actions: { ... },
          getters: { ... },
        },
      },
    },
    moduleB: {
      state: () => ({ ... }),
      mutations: { ... },
      actions: { ... },
```

```
      getters: { ... },
    },
  }
});
```

Here, we've got a store with two root-level modules ('moduleA' and 'moduleB'), and one sub-module ('subModuleA' under 'moduleA').

By default, actions, mutations and getters inside modules are still registered under the global namespace. To make a module to register it under its own local space, you have to set the namespaced property to true in module definition.

```
const store = new Vuex.Store({
  ...
  modules: {
    account: {
      namespaced: true,
      // module assets
      state: () => ({ ... }),
      mutations: { ... },
      actions: { ... },
      getters: { ... },
    }
  }
});
```

The getters, actions and mutations inside a namespaced module are accessed according to the following path rule:

```
store.getters['account/someGetter']; // accessing namespaced getter
store.dispatch('account/someAction'); // dispatching namespaced action
store.commit('account/someMutation'); // committing a namespaced mutation
```

You can also use the mapState, mapGetters, mapActions and map-Mutations helpers with namespace. Here is a simple example:

```
import { mapState, mapActions } from 'vuex'

export default {
  computed: {
    ...mapState('some/nested/module', {
      // this will map this.a to store.state.some.nested.module.a
      a: state => state.a
    })
  },
  methods: {
    ...mapActions('some/nested/module', [
      // this will map this.updateB() to store.dispatch('some/nested/module/
          updateB')
```

```
    'updateB'
  ]),
 }
}
```

This flexibility of module organization in Vuex allows a better code organization and maintenance. You can divide your code into manageable and encapsulated units which helps in building a large application with Vue. Each module can be responsible for a specific aspect of the state and it can be developed and tested in isolation before being wired up into the main application.

4.5   Explain the concept of server-side rendering (SSR) in Vue. Why might you use it?

Server-side rendering (SSR) is a popular technique for rendering a normally client-side only single page app (SPA) on the server and then sending a fully rendered page to the client. Vue.js supports server-side rendering out of the box, which allows your Vue apps to be first executed on the server, and then delivered to client-side for the "hydration" process.

The Vue offers 'vue-server-renderer' package which, combined with Vuex for state management and Vue router, can provide a complete SSR solution.

Here are some reasons why you might use SSR:

1. **Better SEO**: Since search engine crawlers will be able to directly see the fully rendered page. As of now, Google and Bing can index synchronous JavaScript applications just fine. Synchronous being the key word there. If your app starts with a loading spinner, then fetches content via Ajax, the crawler will not wait for you to finish. For other search engines or for certain social media sites like Twitter or LinkedIn, client-rendered or asynchronously fetched content can

be invisible.

2. **Faster time-to-content**: Especially for slow internet or slow devices, server-rendered markup doesn't need to wait until all JavaScript has been downloaded and executed to be displayed, so your user will see a fully-rendered page sooner. This generally results in better user experience, and can be critical for applications where time-to-content is directly associated with the conversion rate.

However, it's also worth mentioning that SSR can be more involved than just client-side rendering (CSR), since there are certain implications:

- Development constraints: Browser-specific code only needs to be executed after mount, this is in contrast to a Vue.js client-side app where we can do it in lifecycle hooks.

- More server-side load: Rendering a full application in Node.js is going to be more CPU-intensive than just serving static files, so if you expect high traffic, be prepared for corresponding server load and wisely employ caching strategies.

- More complexity: SSR would require a Node.js server to be operational, meaning that deploying your application could be a bit more difficult than if it's all handled on the client side.

Here is a simplified Vue SSR example:

```
// Step 1: Create a Vue instance
const Vue = require("vue");
const app = new Vue({
  template: `<div>Hello, {{ msg }}</div>`,
  data: {
    msg: "Vue SSR"
  }
});

// Step 2: Create a renderer
const renderer = require("vue-server-renderer").createRenderer();

// Step 3: Render the Vue instance to HTML
renderer.renderToString(app, (err, html) => {
  if (err) throw err;
  console.log(html);
});
```

This script will output the following HTML string:

```
<div data-server-rendered="true">Hello, Vue SSR</div>
```

With Vue Router and Vuex store the implementation becomes more complex as Vue instance, Router and Store should be instantiated per each request.

For this task Vue recommends using 'vue-router' and 'vuex' modules, that are specifically designed to handle SSR with routing and state management. You can check more detailed guide on the official Vue.js SSR guide.

4.6 How do you optimize a Vue application for performance?

Optimizing a Vue.js application for performance typically involves a combination of tactics that reduce the size of your application and minimize browser computations.

1. Code Splitting: Vue.js allows you to split your code into manageable modules which can then be loaded on demand. This practice known as code-splitting drastically reduces the initial loading time of application. With Vue Router, you can load routes lazily when visited by user.

```
const Foo = () => import('./Foo.vue')
```

2. Using keys in v-for: This makes sure that elements are reused properly in Vue's virtual DOM implementation which can contribute to reducing rendering times. This is because when Vue is updating a list of elements rendered with 'v-for', it uses an algorithm that minimises element movement.

```
<div v-for="(item, index) in items" :key="index">
  <!-- content -->
</div>
```

3. Caching: You can also implement component caching using vue's

built-in <keep-alive> component. This can help to cache already fetched data and avoid unnecessary client-server round trips and computations.

```
<keep-alive>
  <component :is="selectedComponent">
</keep-alive>
```

4. Minimizing and compressing static files: Serve compressed versions of your files and ensure static files are served from the fastest source possible (like a CDN). In the vue config file these settings can be controlled.

5. Preloading and prefetching: Vue gives us two handy annotations — preload and prefetch, which are great for ensuring resources we'll need in future are fetched early on.

6. Component-Level Caching: For components that make AJAX requests upon initial render, you might benefit from component-level caching. Vue provides a mixin entitled vue-async-computed that allows computed properties to depend asynchronously on AJAX data.

Finally, use Devtools performance tab and Google Lighthouse for performance profiling, diagnosis and improvements. This allows you to see which parts of your application are taking the longest to render and can guide your optimization strategies.

4.7 Discuss the role of render functions and when you might use them over templates.

In Vue.js, the primary way of defining the structure of a component is by using HTML-based templates. These templates make it easier for developers to understand and visualize the final output of a component. As a result, templates are excellent for the majority of use cases. However, in situations where developers need more flexibility and control, Vue.js offers an alternative method of defining the structure of a component: the "render" function.

A render function is a Vue.js feature that allows developers to create Vue.js elements, also known as VNodes, programmatically. Instead of writing a template in HTML, a render function makes use of JavaScript to produce Vue.js elements. Render functions aid developers by giving them direct access to JavaScript's powerful features, such as conditionals, loops, and temporary variables.

Now, let's talk about when you might want to use a render function over a template. One scenario is when you need to generate large lists of elements dynamically. Here, render functions can potentially be more efficient because they allow you to control the process more granularly, avoiding unnecessary re-rendering of the whole list when only a few elements change.

Moreover, you might want to use a render function when you want to create high-order components. These are components that accept other components or elements as input, similar to how a function can accept other functions as arguments. Again, a render function can give you more flexibility in how to handle such input compared to a static template.

Here's a simple example how you might use a render function:

```
Vue.component('example', {
  render: function (createElement) {
    return createElement(
      'h1', // tag name
      this.$slots.default // array of children
    )
  }
})
```

This 'example' component, when used like this '<example>Hello world</example>', would produce '<h1>Hello world</h1>'.

To summarize, while templates are often the best choice for declaring the structure of Vue.js components because of their simplicity and readability, render functions offer a powerful alternative for more complex scenarios because they give developers more control over the creation and manipulation of Vue.js elements.

4.8 How do you handle error boundaries in Vue?

Error boundaries feature is unfortunately not directly available in Vue.js like React. However, this doesn't mean we can't handle errors effectively in Vue.js, we can do it through Vue's global error handling mechanism or component level error handling mechanism.

1. **Global Error Handling**

This could be achieved using Vue.config.errorHandler option, which assigns a method to handle any error that occurred anywhere in your Vue application.

Here is an example:

```
Vue.config.errorHandler = function (err, vm, info) {
  // handle error
  // `info` is Vue-specific error info, e.g. which lifecycle hook the error was
      found in
  console.log('An error has occurred: ' + info);
};
```

The error handler receives three arguments:

- 'err': the error itself.

- 'vm': the Vue instance that the error happened in.

- 'info': additional information about the error.

2. **Component Level Error Handling**

Component-level error handling is done through a special instance method, 'errorCaptured'. When an error from any descendant component is captured, this method will be invoked.

Here is an example:

```
export default {
  errorCaptured (err, vm, info) {
    // err: error trace
    // vm: component instance
    // info: which hook the error was found in
    // TODO: handle error
    // if return false, stop propagation
  }
}
```

The 'errorCaptured' hook receives similar arguments to the global error handler, and if the 'errorCaptured' hook returns false, then no other 'errorCaptured' hooks are called after it, and the error is considered to be handled.

These two mechanisms should give you a good level of control over error handling in a Vue.js application. Currently, Vue does not have something exactly equivalent to React's Error Boundaries, instead it provides you different ways to handle errors globally or within a component.

4.9   Describe the differences between functional and stateful components in Vue.

In Vue.js, two primary types of components are used: functional components and stateful (also called non-functional) components. The primary differences between these two types of components boil down to state management, reactivity, and lifecycle hooks.

Functional Components: Functional components in Vue.js are functions with no state, instances, or lifecycle hooks. They are stateless components that receive props as arguments and return a Virtual DOM (VNode).

Here's a representation of a functional component:

```
Vue.component('my-component', {
  functional: true,
```

```
// Props are optional
props: {...},
// To compensate for the lack of `this`,
// we now provide the first argument as the context,
// i.e., an object containing the following properties:
// props, children, slots, scopedSlots, data, parent, ...
render: function (createElement, context) {
  return createElement('div', context.props.myProp)
}
})
```

Functional components are primarily used for presentational purposes where we do not need to manage any internal state or side effects. Due to their simplicity and statelessness, they are more efficient and have faster render times than stateful components.

Stateful Components: Stateful components, on the other hand, are standard Vue components that have state, instances, and lifecycle hooks. They are used in cases where the component has to maintain information, have complex UI logic, or manage side effects.

Here's an example of a stateful component:

```
new Vue({
  el: '#app',
  data: {
    message: 'Hello␣Vue.js!'
  },
  methods: {
    reverseMessage: function () {
      this.message = this.message.split('').reverse().join('')
    }
  }
})
```

In the above example, 'data' is the state of the Vue component. The method 'reverseMessage' changes the state of the component.

A stateful component has a lifecycle like: created, mounted, updated, and destroyed.

Comparing the two, Functional components are faster than Stateful components because they don't have a state, they don't have a reactive system, and they don't have any lifecycle methods. That's why they give a bit of performance improvements when rendering a large number of components. However, Stateful components are more feature-rich, they can take advantage of Vue's reactivity system and have access to Vue's lifecycle hooks. You can decide which type of component to use based on your specific needs in the application.

4.10   How do you integrate TypeScript with Vue?

To integrate TypeScript with Vue.js, you need to set up your Vue project and TypeScript configurations. Here is a step-by-step guide on how to achieve this:

1. Set up your Vue project: You can easily set up a Vue project using Vue CLI. To create a project with TypeScript, specify this during the project creation process by following these steps:

- Install Vue CLI globally in your machine if you haven't done so: 'npm install -g @vue/cli'

- Create a new Vue project: 'vue create my-project-name'. In the prompts section, manually select features and then choose 'TypeScript'.

2. Set up TypeScript configurations: The TypeScript configuration file 'tsconfig.json' is generated automatically when you create your Vue project with TypeScript. However, you may sometimes have to manually adjust the configuration to suit your specific needs. Here's what a basic 'tsconfig.json' file often looks like:

```
{
  "compilerOptions": {
    "target": "es5",
    "module": "es2015",
    "strict": true,
    "moduleResolution": "node",
    "experimentalDecorators": true,
    "esModuleInterop": true,
    "allowSyntheticDefaultImports": true,
    "sourceMap": true,
    "baseUrl": ".",
    "paths": {
      "@/*": [
        "src/*"
```

```
    ]
  },
  "lib": [
    "es2017",
    "dom"
  ]
},
"include": [
  "src/**/*.ts",
  "src/**/*.vue"
],
"exclude": [
  "node_modules"
]
}
```

The setting 'experimentalDecorators' must be turned on for Vue to properly work with TypeScript. We include 'vue' files in the 'tsconfig.json' because we want TypeScript to process '.vue' single file components.

3. Using TypeScript in your Vue components: Once the configurations are set, we can start writing Vue components using TypeScript. Here's an example of a simple Vue component with TypeScript:

```
<template>
  <div>{{ message }}</div>
</template>

<script lang="ts">
import { Vue, Component, Prop } from 'vue-property-decorator';

@Component
export default class HelloWorld extends Vue {
  message: string = 'Hello, Vue with TypeScript!'
}
</script>
```

As seen in this example, we use 'vue-property-decorator' for the class-style syntax. This is much recommended for use alongside TypeScript.

Remember, TypeScript support in Vue is incrementally adoptable and it's totally fine to partly apply TypeScript in a Vue project.

4. Use TypeScript for Vuex: For global state management with Vuex, TypeScript can also be integrated. You simply declare your state like so:

```
interface State {
  count: number
}

const store: StoreOptions<State> = {
  state: {
    count: 0
  },
  // other options ...
}
```

To summarize, integrating TypeScript into a Vue project requires
you to set up your Vue project with TypeScript support and ensure
your TypeScript configuration is properly set. Then you would write
Vue components with TypeScript and optionally apply TypeScript
for Vuex as well.

4.11   Explain the Vue 3 Composition API. How does it compare to the Options API?

The Vue 3 Composition API is a new feature introduced in Vue 3 that
allows developers to encapsulate and reuse logic across components.
It is introduced alongside the classic Options API to address some of
the limitations that the Options API had traditionally.

Composition API introduces a setup function where we can use reactive state, watchers, computed properties, lifecycle hooks and organize
them in the way we like.

Here is an example of how to use reactive variables with the Composition API:

```
import { reactive } from 'vue'

export default {
  setup() {
    const state = reactive({
      count: 0
    })

    return {
```

```
    state
  }
 }
}
```

Now let's compare the Composition API to the Options API:

1. Options API divides code based on option types: 'data', 'methods', 'watch', 'computed', 'props', 'lifecycle hooks' etc. which might be good for small to medium sized projects.

2. Composition API organizes code by logical concern. You can group code by functionality rather than by the Vue feature. This can make the code much easier to manage in larger applications or when dealing with complex features.

3. Vue Options API can have some drawbacks with TypeScript support, while the Composition API is more friendly with TypeScript.

4. With Vue Options API, reusing and organizing code logic would require mix-ins, which can introduce naming conflicts and cause difficulties in terms of readability and maintainability. However, Composition API can extract and reuse logic through functions, rendering it more maintainable and readable.

5. Composition API can provide better performance optimisations, since you can control what internal state can get reactive.

Here, it is notable that Composition API is not meant to replace the Options API, which is a great solution for smaller applications or components. They are both available for use in Vue.js and can be chosen based on the use case.

Here's how you would define a component with the Options API:

```
export default {
  props: ['id'],
  data () {
    return {
      user: null
    }
  },
  created () {
```

```
  axios.get(`/api/users/${this.id}`).then(response => {
    this.user = response.data
  })
 }
}
```

And here's how you would do it using the Composition API:

```
export default {
  props: ['id'],
  setup (props) {
    const user = ref(null)
    onMounted(async () => {
      const response = await axios.get(`/api/users/${props.id}`)
      user.value = response.data
    })

    return {
      user
    }
  }
}
```

As you can see, the Composition API has a different approach to organization and reusability compared to the Options API, offering more flexibility in organizing code. That being said, it's always important to take into consideration the specific needs and requirements of the project when deciding which approach to use.

4.12   How do you handle internationalization (i18n) in a Vue application?

Handling internationalization (i18n) in Vue.js applications can be achieved by utilizing the vue-i18n library.

The vue-i18n library integrates seamlessly with Vue.js applications, providing a comprehensive API that you can tie into your application lifecycle. It also allows to dynamically switch between different locales and offers a simple syntax for your templates.

The first step to achieve internationalization in Vue.js is to install vue-i18n:

```
npm install vue-i18n
```

After installation, you need to configure it in your Vue app:

```
import Vue from 'vue'
import VueI18n from 'vue-i18n'

Vue.use(VueI18n)

const messages = {
  en: {
    message: {
      hello: 'hello world'
    }
  },
  fr: {
    message: {
      hello: 'Bonjour le monde'
    }
  }
}
const i18n = new VueI18n({
  locale: 'en', // set locale
  messages, // set locale messages
})

new Vue({
  i18n,
  render: h => h(App)
}).$mount('#app')
```

In this example, we define a bunch of messages in different languages (English and French in this case). These are provided to an instance of the VueI18n class. The 'messages' key takes an object, where the keys are language codes and the values are translation dictionaries.

Using vue-i18n on Vue.js templates is easy:

```
<h1>{{ $t('message.hello') }}</h1>
```

The '$t()' method is used to switch translation strings. The argument to the method is a path to a translation string in the messages object. Note that paths are defined as keys in the object tree, and are fetched relative to the root. For example ''message.hello'' refers to the 'hello' property in the 'message' object.

You can change the current locale dynamically, by changing the 'locale' property of the 'i18n' object:

```
// switch to French
this.$i18n.locale = 'fr'
```

This will automatically change all displayed messages that use vue-i18n. Note that you should ensure that all locales are loaded and available before you switch to them.

Vue-i18n also offers full support for component-level localization, number formatting, date formatting, handling of pluralization rules, and a number of other features. This makes vue-i18n very suitable for any size of application, from small widgets to large scale applications with several different languages.

4.13   Describe the use of custom directives in Vue. Provide an example.

Custom directives are very useful in Vue.js when you wish to reuse code throughout your application. A directive provides a way to extend Vue instances and components with custom behavior. It allows you to create reusable code that can manage various instances of Vue, with the ability to bind Vue instances and components to certain DOM-related behaviors.

The custom directives in Vue.js provide a more semantic and reusable way to control the behavior of certain components, especially when dealing with direct DOM manipulation.

Directives in Vue.js have several hooks:

1. 'bind': This is called only once, when the directive is first bound to the element.

2. 'inserted': This is called when the bound element has been inserted into its parent node.

3. 'update': This is called when the component has been updated,

but before its children have been updated.

4. 'componentUpdated': This is called after the component and its children have been updated.

5. 'unbind': This is called only once, when the directive is unbound from the element.

Here is an example to illustrate the use of a custom directive. Suppose you want to create a directive that automatically sets color and font size of a text.

```
Vue.directive('my-directive', {
  bind: function(el, binding, vnode) {
    //el is the actual element the directive was bound to.
    //We can directly manipulate the element using the native DOM APIs.
    el.style.color = binding.value.color;
    el.style.fontSize = binding.value.size;
  },
  update: function(el, binding, vnode, oldVnode) {
    //this will be called when the bound property's data changes.
    el.style.color = binding.value.color;
  }
});
```

To use this directive:

```
<div v-my-directive="{ color: 'red', size: '20px' }">Hello!</div>
```

This makes it easy to reuse the same piece of DOM manipulation across multiple Vue instances and components.

Please note that it's a good practice to keep your directives as simple as possible to improve readability and maintainability of your code. Complex logic should rather be moved to methods or computed properties.

4.14   How do you handle security concerns, such as XSS attacks, in a Vue application?

Ensuring security in Vue.js application is crucial, there are few strategies and best practices to handle security concerns, such as Cross-Site Scripting (XSS) attacks.

1. **Escape HTML input:** XSS attacks involve the injection of malicious code into your application, typically through form inputs. Vue.js automatically escapes HTML content in mustache bindings and expressions. Therefore, HTML code entered in your form inputs will be displayed as text and will not be executed as code.

```
<!-- Vue.js escapes the HTML code -->
<span v-html="userInput"></html>

<!-- Raw HTML -->
<!-- userInput = <img src='http://url.to.file.which/not.exist' onerror=alert(
    document.cookie);> -->
<!-- this will be interpreted as text, not HTML, preventing the XSS attack -->
<span>{{ userInput }}</span>
```

2. **Limit use of v-html:** 'v-html' is a Vue directive that can be used to output HTML in your templates. However, beware that the use of 'v-html' makes your code more vulnerable to XSS attacks, as it can interpret and execute injected JavaScript code. If you have to use 'v-html', always ensure that the injected content comes from a trustworthy and sanitized source.

3. **Use Content Security Policy (CSP):** CSP is an additional layer of security that helps to detect and mitigate certain types of attacks, including Cross Site Scripting (XSS). It puts restrictions on the content that can be loaded on your website and helps reduce the risk of XSS attacks.

4. **Use HTTPOnly cookies:** Cross-site scripting attack also extends to stealing cookies. Making a cookie HTTPOnly will protect it from being accessed through client-side JavaScript.

In Vue.js, we don't manipulate the DOM directly, so we avoid most of these problems. However, it's crucial to always keep security concerns in mind, especially when dealing with user-provided content, and to apply best coding practices to mitigate potential threats.

4.15 Discuss the role of dependency injection in Vue using provide and inject.

Dependency Injection is a critical aspect in Vue.js, especially when it comes to dealing with component communication. It helps transfer data or methods from a given component to its descendants regardless of how deep the component hierarchy is. This is particularly useful when you have a lot of nested child components and passing props down the chain would be too difficult or messy.

Vue.js uses the 'provide' and 'inject' options for dependency injection.

Here's how it works:

1. 'Provide':

The 'provide' option should be an object or a function which returns an object. This object contains the properties that are available for injection into its descendants. You add the 'provide' option in the parent component where you declare your data or methods to provide.

```
// Parent component
export default {
  provide: {
    foo: 'bar',
    hello: function() {
      return 'world';
    }
  }
}
```

2. 'Inject':

In the descendants, you use the 'inject' option to start using the provided data. The 'inject' option should be an array of strings or an object where the strings are the keys provided by 'provide'.

```
// Child component
export default {
  inject: ['foo', 'hello'],
  mounted() {
    console.log(this.foo) // "bar"
    console.log(this.hello()) // "world"
  }
}
```

In this example, 'foo' and 'hello' from the parent component are injected into the child component. The names must match exactly to those provided by 'provide'.

Note that unlike 'props', 'provide' and 'inject' do not create a direct contract between the components. This means when you change 'foo' or 'hello' in the child component, it's not reflected in the parent component.

The 'provide/inject' feature is particularly suited for developing plugin-like features, as these properties injection are deep into all descendant components, virtually regardless of how deep. It's an advanced feature and should be used wisely.

4.16   How do you handle code splitting in a Vue application?

Code splitting in Vue.js is a technique used for a more optimal loading of the application by splitting the app into multiple output files that can be dynamically loaded at runtime. This helps to reduce the size of the main JavaScript file that needs to be loaded initially, and allows specific functionalities to be loaded as needed, giving an overall boost to performance. This feature can be especially useful for large scale applications where you don't need to load all the routes and its related components at once.

Vue.js offers an easy way to implement code splitting using dynamic imports in combination with Vue's asynchronous component syntax.

Here's a basic example of how you can use dynamic imports for a route component:

```
const About = () => import(/* webpackChunkName: "about" */ './About.vue')

export default [
  { path: '/about', component: About }
]
```

In this case, the "About" page component will be loaded only when the user navigates to "/about".

This technique can similarly be applied to lazy load other Vue components. Here's an example:

```
export default {
  components: {
    MyComponent: () => import(/* webpackChunkName: "my-component" */ './
        MyComponent.vue')
  }
}
```

By using 'import()' instead of 'import', Webpack will automatically split your code into separate bundles which will be loaded over Ajax requests.

Vue CLI has this feature out of the box as it uses Webpack to bundle the application. The comment 'webpackChunkName: "about"' is used to group components into the same chunk. This gives you more control over which components are grouped together resulting in less code duplication.

One of the challenges with code splitting is to ensure that all parts of your application have been loaded correctly and are available when needed. This can be achieved by using Vue router's 'beforeResolve' or 'beforeEnter' navigation guards.

Remember that code splitting should be used judiciously and tested thoroughly to ensure that it does not introduce new performance or other issues.

4.17   Explain the concept of dynamic module registration in Vuex.

Dynamic module registration in Vuex allows you to register a module after the store has been created. This capability is especially useful for large scale applications where different parts of the application can load or unload modules dynamically based on the need.

The main advantage is, it allows you to break down your store into modules, each with its own state, mutations, actions, and getters. This contributes to better organization of your code, making it easier to manage state.

To register a module dynamically, you can use the 'registerModule' method. Here's an example:

```
store.registerModule('myModule', {
  // state
  state: () => ({
    customField: 'This is custom'
  }),
  // mutations
  mutations: {
    updateField (state, payload) {
      state.customField = payload;
    }
  },
})
```

In the example above, "myModule" is the name we're giving to this module. We're also defining a custom state field within this module called "customField", and a mutation that allows us to update "customField".

You can later unregister this module using the 'unregisterModule' method.

```
store.unregisterModule('myModule');
```

Note: While the module is alive, all of its state is added to the store's root state, all getters are added to the store's root getters, and actions and mutations are added to the global namespace.

Besides, Vuex allows us to have module reuse, thanks to function state and module encapsulation. It also supports nested modules which allows state management to be divided into small maintainable parts.

4.18   How do you synchronize Vue Router's state with Vuex?

We can synchronize the Vue Router state with Vuex using the module 'vuex-router-sync'. The 'vuex-router-sync' library creates a Vuex module that keeps the state of Vue Router sync with Vuex. This makes it possible to mutate the router's current path from the Vuex store.

To use this library, you need to install it first using npm:

```
npm install vuex-router-sync
```

Here's a step by step process on how you can do this:

Step 1: Import the 'vuex-router-sync' library, Vue Router and Vuex.

```
import { sync } from 'vuex-router-sync';
import VueRouter from 'vue-router';
import Vuex from 'vuex';
```

Step 2: Initialize the Vue Router and Vuex Store.

```
const router = new VueRouter({ ... });
const store = new Vuex.Store({ ... });
```

Step 3: Call the 'sync' function and pass the 'store' and 'router' to it.

```
sync(store, router);
```

This way the 'route' object in your Vuex store's state will always be a copy of your current route. This 'route' object contains:

- 'path': current path (string),
- 'params': current params (object),
- 'query': current query (object),
- 'name': current route name (string, if named routes used).

It allows you to fully control the router from your Vuex actions. Also, when you mutate the Vuex state to change the route the URL and the displayed component will be updated to match the new route.

For example, you can commit mutation to navigate to a new URL:

```
store.commit('router/ROUTE_CHANGED', { path: '/new-path' });
```

or dispatch an action:

```
store.dispatch('router/goTo', '/new-path');
```

Both 'commit' and 'dispatch' will lead to changing the current route to "/new-path".

Remember, this is an advanced feature. You should only do this kind of synchronization when you really need it - it can be overkill for small apps or if you don't need to access routing data directly from your Vuex Store. In most cases, Vue Router alone is enough to manage the routing for your Vue application.

4.19   Describe the differences and use cases for keep-alive in Vue.

'<keep-alive>' is a built-in abstract component in Vue.js that is used to keep dynamic components in memory to preserve state and avoid re-rendering. This component is particularly useful in situations where you may want to preserve component state or avoid re-rendering for performance reasons.

Here are some primary differences and use cases for '<keep-alive>' in Vue:

1. **Without using '<keep-alive>':**

When you switch between components, the state of the component gets destroyed, and Vue.js creates a new one when the component is needed again. This process can be inefficient, especially for components that involve complex computations, API calls, or contain larger nested structures, as they would need to be re-rendered and re-created each time the component is loaded.

2. **Using '<keep-alive>':**

'<keep-alive>' prevents destroying the component state when switching. Instead, it caches the state of the component and allows the component to be reloaded faster when needed again, as it avoids the cost of re-rendering the component. For example, it can be useful in a tab-based interface where switching between tabs should preserve the state of the tabs and not re-render them.

Here is a simple use case using '<keep-alive>' component:

```
<template>
  <div>
    <button @click="show␣=␣!show">Toggle</button>

    <keep-alive>
      <hello-world v-if="show" />
    </keep-alive>
  </div>
</template>

<script>
import HelloWorld from './HelloWorld.vue'

export default {
  components: {
    HelloWorld
  },
  data () {
    return {
      show: true
    }
  }
}
```

```
</script>
```

In this example, the '<HelloWorld>' component is toggled to be shown or hidden when the button is clicked. Without '<keep-alive>', each time the component is shown, Vue.js would have to re-render the '<HelloWorld>' component from scratch. With '<keep-alive>', Vue.js caches the component and keeps the state, allowing the component to be shown quicker when it's needed again, and preserving the component's state between toggles.

Apart from simply wrapping the component, '<keep-alive>' also has some advanced features, like the 'include' and 'exclude' attributes to control which components to cache or skip. In addition, it provides two lifecycle hooks 'activated' and 'deactivated' which are called when the component is loaded into and removed from the cache respectively.

4.20   How do you handle server-push events, like WebSockets, in a Vue application?

Managing real-time server-push events such as WebSockets in a Vue.js application can be achieved by combining the use of Vuex for state management and a WebSocket client. Here's how you would generally handle it:

1. **Creating the WebSocket client**: First, you need to set up the WebSocket client. You can use native WebSocket API or libraries such as socket.io-client to create a connection to your server which supports WebSocket.

```
const socket = new WebSocket('ws://your-websocket-server')
```

2. **Listening to server events**: After successfully creating a WebSocket instance, you can now listen to server events. WebSocket API provides several event handlers including 'onopen', 'onmessage', 'on-

close', 'onerror'. Most importantly, you would listen to 'onmessage' events which are triggered whenever a message is received from the server.

```
socket.onmessage = function(event) {
  console.log(event.data)
}
```

3. **Integration with Vuex**: To make your application reactive to these server-push events, you'd typically want to dispatch Vuex actions within these event handlers. These actions can commit mutations and change the state of your Vue application. Let's assume that you want to update a 'messages' array in your Vuex state every time a message event is received:

```
// In your WebSocket event handlers
socket.onmessage = function(event) {
  // Assume that 'store' is your Vuex store instance
  store.dispatch('addMessage', event.data)
}

// And in your Vuex store
const store = new Vuex.Store({
  state: {
    messages: []
  },
  mutations: {
    ADD_MESSAGE(state, payload) {
      state.messages.push(payload)
    }
  },
  actions: {
    addMessage({ commit }, message) {
      commit('ADD_MESSAGE', message)
    }
  }
})
```

In the Vue components, you can then use mapState helper to make your component reactive to these state changes.

```
// In your Vue components
computed: {
  ...Vuex.mapState(['messages'])
}
```

4. **Error handling and reconnection**: You also need to handle connection errors and potentially implement a reconnection strategy

in case the connection to your server is lost. You could do this in the 'onerror' and 'onclose' event handlers.

Note: It is a good practice to encapsulate all the WebSocket code into a separate service or plugin, so that it can be easily mocked for test, reused in your application, and does not mix with your component's code.

Chapter 5

Expert

5.1 How do you handle large-scale state management in Vue applications without relying solely on Vuex?

To handle state management in a large-scale Vue application without solely relying on Vuex, developers can apply the following concepts:

1. **Event Bus**: This is where you create an empty Vue instance and use it as a central event bus. You can emit an event in one component and listen for that event in another component. This helps you keep your components decoupled while still communicating with each other.

Example:

```
// the event bus
var bus = new Vue()

// emitting an event from a component
bus.$emit('my-event', myData)
```

```
// listening for an event in another component
bus.$on('my-event', handleMyEvent)
```

2. **Props / Custom Events**: A child component can emit an event, and the parent component can then listen to that event and react accordingly. This is a built-in mechanism in Vue.js for parent-child communication. Also, via Props, child components can receive data from parent components, ensuring data flow only one way, from parent to child.

3. **Provide / Inject**: Introduced in Vue 2.2.0+, the 'provide' and 'inject' options provide an advanced way to build hierarchical dependency injection systems which can be beneficial when you want to pass data from a higher-level component to a deeper-level component without having to pass the data through all the component layers in between. Note: this should be used sparingly considering it couples components close together.

Example:

```
// an ancestor component using "provide"
provide: {
  myData: 'This is my data'
}

// a descendant component using "inject"
inject: ['myData'],
created() {
  console.log(this.myData) // "This is my data"
}
```

4. **Local Storage / Session Storage**: These are Web Storage API methods that allow you to store data on the user's browser. Depending on the data type, sensitivity, and duration it needs to be stored, one of these methods may be more appropriate to use than the other.

5. **Backend API**: A backend API plays the pivotal role of retrieving, storing, and sending data for large-scale applications. It allows components throughout the application to make requests for the same information.

Remember that as stated by Vue's style guide, Vuex should be used in complex, large-scale state management cases. It could be helpful on the long run for maintaining the application.

5.2 Discuss the internal workings of the virtual DOM diffing algorithm in Vue.

Vue.js uses a virtual DOME diffing algorithm to determine the minimum amount of changes necessary to update the real DOM in order to effectively display the current state of the application. This algorithm is a key part of Vue's reactive UI approach and contributes significantly to its performance.

Here's a high-level overview of how Vue's virtual DOM diffing algorithm works:

1. **Creation of the virtual DOM tree**: Vue first builds a virtual DOM tree. When a state change happens, instead of directly making changes to the DOM, Vue creates a new virtual DOM tree.

2. **Comparison of the new virtual DOM with the old one**: The new virtual DOM tree is then compared with the old one. Only the differences between the two trees are computed. This is done with a "diffing" algorithm.

3. **Patch process**: The differences are then patched to the real DOM. For every new state, Vue performs the minimal number of DOM manipulations possible to actually update the UI to reflect the new state.

The diffing algorithm works in two steps:

- **Node diffing**: Vue walks through the tree of elements (nodes) and checks if the same node is present in both trees. It uses heuristic techniques like comparing tag names and keys to quickly identify similar nodes. If it finds a node that differs, it replaces the old node entirely.

- **Children diffing**: Once Vue has determined that two nodes are the same, it will then compare the children of the nodes to each other. Here, Vue.js uses an algorithm that checks key-based nodes first, as these can be moved instead of deleted/created, which has better performance.

Here's an example for better understanding:

```
// Old VNode
const oldVNode = h('div', [h('p', 'hello')])

// New VNode
const newVNode = h('div', [h('p', 'goodbye')])

// Patch Old VNode with new VNode
patch(oldVNode, newVNode)
```

In this scenario, Vue's diffing algorithm will first compare the 'div' nodes, then it will compare their children ('p' nodes), and finally update the text content from 'hello' to 'goodbye'.

This process is efficient and provides high performance, leading to faster and smoother UI updates. The 'diff' and 'patch' operations work together to ensure the smallest possible manipulations to the DOM. This allows Vue.js to be very fast, even for large scale applications.

5.3   How would you implement server-side hydration in a Vue SSR setup?

Server-side rendering (SSR) in Vue.js allows your Vue app to be rendered on the server, send HTML to the browser, and then "hydrate" that static markup into a fully functional app on the client-side. This is especially useful for improving the initial load performance and SEO of your Vue application.

Here's a high-level overview of how you would implement server-side hydration in a Vue.js SSR setup:

1. **Setup Vue SSR:** You begin by setting up Vue SSR according to the Vue SSR guide.

2. **Create Vue Instance:** On the server, we create a new Vue instance for each request.

```
const app = new Vue({
  render: h => h(App)
});
```

3. **Render Vue Instance to string:** We then use 'renderer.renderToString(app)' to render that Vue instance into a string. In this step, Vue renders the entire app to static HTML and sends it to the browser.

```
renderer.renderToString(app, (err, html) => {
  if (err) throw err
  console.log(html)
  // => <div data-server-rendered="true">Hello World</div>
})
```

4. **Inject result into HTML Page:** We insert this rendered string into our HTML skeleton where we want our app to mount.

```
<html>
  <body>
    <div id="app"><!--vue-ssr-outlet--></div>
  </body>
</html>
```

5. **Client-side hydration:** On the client-side, instead of creating a new app and mounting it to our div, we instead want Vue to "hydrate" the existing HTML that was rendered by the server.

This is done by using 'Vue.mount('#app', true)' on the client side. The second argument of 'true' tells Vue that it should perform hydration instead of a full re-render.

```
new Vue({
  el: '#app'
});
```

Vue will preserve all the existing DOM elements, attach event handlers, and establish reactivity for data. From now on, the application behaves just like a completely client-side rendered Vue app.

It's important to note that the server-side rendered HTML should be a valid representation of the same state described by the client-side app, otherwise, hydration will fail. The data used for rendering the app on the server should be the same data that is used on the client-side.

That's why it's recommended to use a Vue data store like Vuex to manage your application state, as it's designed to work well with SSR and hydration. You can populate your Vuex store with data on the server, and then have the client-side code leverage the same Vuex store state to ensure successful hydration.

```
store.replaceState(window.__INITIAL_STATE__)
const app = new Vue({
  store,
  render: h => h(App)
})
```

Where 'window.___INITIAL_STATE___' would be your server-rendered state. In this way, any state changes that happen on the server will also happen on the client, ensuring that hydration succeeds.

5.4   Describe the challenges and solutions for SEO optimization in Single Page Applications (SPAs) using Vue.

Single Page Applications (SPAs) are applications that load a single HTML page and dynamically update that page as the user interacts with the app. Vue.js is a popular framework for building SPAs.

Despite the conveniences that SPAs offer, there are a few challenges that developers might face regarding SEO (Search Engine Optimization) with SPAs like Vue.js:

1. ***JavaScript Execution***: By default, search engines crawl and

index static HTML pages. But with SPAs, the content on a webpage is usually rendered with JavaScript, and this may cause issues with search engine crawlers not being able to properly index the page's content.

2. ***Dealing with Async operations***: SPAs usually wait for some data before they render the content, e.g., fetching data from an API. The crawler may not wait for this data and might index an empty page.

3. ***Difficulties in setting Meta tags***: Generally, relevant meta tags for SEO purposes are set server-side. However, given that SPAs are predominantly client-side, this can be a challenge.

Solutions:

1. ***Server-Side Rendering (SSR)***: You can use SSR to deliver an application in a fully rendered, text-rich format to your users and search engine spiders. SSR means rendering the SPA on the server and sending a fully rendered page to the client. Vue.js supports SSR using 'vue-server-renderer' package. SSR can solve the problem of not only the SEO but also the initial load time that is necessary for many SPAs. For instance:

```
var Vue = require("vue");
var server = require("express")();
var renderer = require("vue-server-renderer").createRenderer();

server.get("*", (req, res) => {
  var app = new Vue({
    data: {
      url: req.url
    },
    template: `<div>The visited URL is: {{ url }}</div>`
  });

  renderer.renderToString(app, (err, html) => {
    if (err) {
      res.status(500).end("Internal␣Server␣Error");
      return;
    }
    res.end(`
      <!DOCTYPE html>
      <html lang="en">
        <body>
          ${html}
        </body>
      </html>
```

```
    `);
  });
});

server.listen(8080);
```

2. ***Pre-rendering***: Another solution can be Pre-rendering which
means generating static HTML pages for routes at build time. It's
useful when you have a relatively small, static website. Vue.js allows
this by using pre-rendering tools such as PrerenderSPAPlugin.

3. ***Dynamic Rendering***: Dynamic Rendering means switching
between client-side rendered and pre-rendered content for certain user
agents. Google Search recommends dynamic rendering, specifically
for websites with a large, ever-changing number of URLs.

4. ***Using 'vue-meta' to handle Meta tags***: 'vue-meta' is a Vue.js
plugin that allows you to manage your app's meta information. Better
SEO requires properly formatted meta tags. Vue-meta allows you to
handle meta tags for each of your Vue.js components:

```
new Vue({
  el: '#app',
  data: {
    msg: 'Hello,␣world!'
  },
  metaInfo: {
    // if no subcomponents specify a metaInfo.title, this title will be used
    title: 'Default␣Title',
    // all titles will be injected into this template
    titleTemplate: '%s␣|␣My␣App'
  }
})
```

Keep in mind, however, that while these solutions can help improve
the SEO of your Vue.js app, they cannot guarantee SEO success.
SEO is a complex field that involves many different factors, and you
should always consult with an SEO expert or do your research before
making any substantial changes to your website.

5.5 How do you optimize reactivity for large datasets in Vue?

Vue's reactivity system is highly efficient and works well out of the box in most scenarios. However, when dealing with large datasets, there can be performance bottlenecks due to the way Vue tracks dependencies of computed properties or watchers, which makes every component reactive. Luckily, there are various techniques to optimize reactivity for large datasets in Vue:

1. **Object.freeze:** Vue.js adds getter and setter pairs to every property of an object for reactivity purposes. In case of large datasets, this can slow down your application considerably. Object.freeze() can be applied to prevent Vue from adding reactivity to the objects. This makes sense if you know that a dataset will not change.

In practical code:

```
data() {
  return {
    largeData: Object.freeze(largeDataset)
  }
}
```

2. **Use functional components:** Functional components are stateless and instanceless, they don't have a reactive data property or life cycle methods. They can re-render very quickly and as such are recommended in situations where a lot of components will be created and destroyed in a short time.

3. **Pagination, virtual scrolling, or lazy loading:** Instead of loading a huge dataset all at once, it might be more efficient to only load a small portion of the data and then load more when it's needed. This can be achieved through pagination, or creating a "virtual" scroll, where only visible data is rendered and as user scrolls, non-visible data is un-rendered and new data is added.

4. **Avoid unnecessary v-binds or computed properties:** You should avoid using v-bind or v-model on components or elements that do not

need reactivity. The more properties Vue has to track, the slower the reactivity system becomes. Instead of computing properties for every data change, use local variables or methods.

5. **Use Vuex for state management:** For complex applications where a lot of components share the same state, Vuex can help to structure your code better and prevent unnecessary re-renders.

Remember, before applying these optimizations, you should always validate if there's a performance problem first (for example, by using Vue DevTools), and only then apply the optimization techniques if needed. Optimization adds complexity, so it should be applied only when necessary.

5.6   Discuss the intricacies of handling complex animations and transitions in Vue.

In Vue.js, animations and transitions are not an afterthought or a separate library, but rather a part of the core library. Vue provides several different ways to apply dynamic transition effects to elements and components when they are inserted, updated, or removed from the DOM.

1. **Vue's Transition Wrapper Component**: Vue provides a '<transition>' wrapper component, allowing you to add entering/leaving transitions for any element or component in the following contexts:

- Conditional rendering (using 'v-if')

- Conditional display (using 'v-show')

- Dynamic components

- Component root nodes

Here is a simple example of a fade transition:

```
<transition name="fade">
  <p v-if="show">Hello Vue.js</p>
```

```
</transition>
```

```
.fade-enter-active, .fade-leave-active {
  transition: opacity .5s;
}
.fade-enter, .fade-leave-to /* .fade-leave-active below version 2.1.8 */ {
  opacity: 0;
}
```

2. **Transition Classes**: Vue automatically applies transition classes and adds appropriate prefixes, triggering CSS transitions or animations. There are six classes applied for enter/leave transitions.

- 'v-enter': Starting state for enter. Added before element is inserted, removed one frame after element is inserted.

- 'v-enter-active': Active state for enter. Applied during the entire entering phase. Added before element is inserted, removed when transition/animation finishes.

- 'v-enter-to': Only available in versions 2.1.8+. Ending state for enter. Added one frame after element is inserted, removed when transition/animation finishes.

- 'v-leave': Starting state for leave. Added immediately when a leaving transition is triggered, removed after one frame.

- 'v-leave-active': Active state for leave. Applied during the entire leaving phase. Added immediately when leave transition is triggered, removed when transition/animation finishes.

- 'v-leave-to': Only available in versions 2.1.8+. Ending state for leave. Added one frame after a leaving transition is triggered, removed when the transition/animation finishes.

3. **JavaScript Hooks**: Vue.js provides hooks for JavaScript animations. You can use third-party animation libraries as well. Vue provides several JavaScript hooks that you can use:

- beforeEnter

- enter

- afterEnter

- enterCancelled

- beforeLeave

- leave

- afterLeave

- leaveCancelled

```
<transition
    @before-enter="beforeEnter"
    @enter="enter"
    @after-enter="afterEnter"
    @enter-cancelled="enterCancelled"
    @before-leave="beforeLeave"
    @leave="leave"
    @after-leave="afterLeave"
    @leave-cancelled="leaveCancelled"
>
    <!-- ... -->
</transition>
```

4. **Transitions on initial render**: If you also want to apply a transition on the initial render of a node, you can add the 'appear' attribute:

```
<transition appear>
    <!-- ... -->
</transition>
```

5. **Transition Group**: The '<transition-group>' component is used to manage transitions for groups of items. It can be used to create complex animations, like list shuffling.

Vue.js provides powerful native techniques to handle animations and transitions, but for handling complex scenarios it's preferred to use third-party libraries like Greensock or Anime.js. The important thing when choosing a library is to ensure it's compatible with Vue's reactive system.

5.7 How do you implement middleware in Vue Router?

Vue Router does not provide a direct feature for middleware, but we can use Navigation Guards, aka "route guards" to incorporate middleware-like behaviors.

There are different types of Navigation Guards:

- Global Before Guards

- Per-Route Guard

- In-Component Guards

Global Before Guards This is a global middleware that will run before every route:

```
router.beforeEach((to, from, next) => {
  // This is your middleware
  next()
})
```

Per-Route Guard If you want to run middleware only for specific paths, you can use '"beforeEnter"':

```
const router = new VueRouter({
  routes: [
    {
      path: '/path',
      component: Component,
      beforeEnter: (to, from, next) => {
      // This is your middleware
      next()
    }
  }
  ]
})
```

In-Component Guards These are more component specific, unlike global middleware which will be run on every route and middleware applied on routes:

```
export default {
  beforeRouteEnter(to, from, next) {
```

```
    // This is your middleware
    next()
  }
}
```

In all the above cases, the middleware function receives three arguments:

- '"to"': The Target route object being navigated to.

- '"from"': The Current route being navigated away from.

- '"next"': This function must be called to resolve the hook. The action depends on the arguments provided to 'next'.

The usage of these arguments might look like this:

```
router.beforeEach((to, from, next) => {
  if (to.path === '/user' && !isLoggedIn()) {
    next('/login')
  } else {
    next()
  }
})
```

In this example, if the targeted path is '/user' and the user is not logged in (determined by 'isLoggedIn()' function), the 'next' function is called with the '/login' path, and the application will navigate to the Login page. If the user is logged in, just calling 'next()' will continue the navigation to the targeted route.

5.8   Explain the potential pitfalls of using mixins and how to avoid them.

Mixins in Vue.js are a flexible way to distribute reusable functionalities for Vue components. You can encapsulate a set of functionalities in one mixin and use it in multiple Vue components. However, using mixins can also bring several potential pitfalls.

1.   **Namespace Clashes:** When integrating mixins that utilize

method names or data properties, collisions might crop up if the names clash. This challenge occurs when the mixin has a method or a data property with the same name as the target component.

How to Avoid: To avoid this, you can use unique and descriptive names for each method and data properties. Name your methods and data properties in a way that describes their function, and prefix the names with the mixin's name.

2. **Difficulty in Identifying Where the Behavior is Coming From:** With many mixins in a Component, it can become unclear which mixin introduces which functionality or property. This makes debugging or maintaining the codebase hard.

How to Avoid: Proper documentation and commenting your code can make it easier to understand where the behavior is coming from. Naming conventions can also help to a good extent.

3. **Implicit Coupling:** If a mixin depends on a method or data property from another mixin or a core component, this creates an implicit coupling, which can make the code difficult to understand, and also create hard-to-track bugs.

How to Avoid: It is better to avoid dependencies between mixins. You should strive to make every mixin independent or encapsulated. If your design truly requires shared state or behavior, you should be explicit about it, and consider using Vuex (Vue's state management pattern and library) instead.

4. **Complexity and Side Effects:** Too many mixins in a component can lead to increased complexity and unexpected side effects, especially when mixins modify the Vue instance.

How to Avoid: Regular refactoring of your Vue.js components and mixins can help keep complexity under control. Try to keep your mixins small, with a single responsibility. Don't add behavior to a mixin unless it's needed by every component that uses the mixin.

Here is the key takeaway: Mixins serve a powerful purpose in Vue.js, by offering a flexible way to build reusable code snippets. However, when used irresponsibly, they can cause more troubles than they solve. Carefully design and implement your mixins to overcome the potential pitfalls.

5.9   How would you handle cross-component communication without using Vuex or an event bus?

Vue.js provides several ways of handling cross-component communication without using Vuex or an Event Bus. Here are two of the most commonly used methods:

1.   **Props and Events**: This approach is simple and it's built directly into Vue.js. The idea here is that you can pass data from a parent component to a child component via props, and then the child component can inform the parent component of changes via events.

Here's a basic example:

```
// Child Component
Vue.component('child-component', {
  props: ['message'],
  template: '<div>{{ message }}</div>',
  methods: {
    updateMessage: function() {
      this.$emit('message-updated', 'New Message')
    }
  }
})

// Parent Component
Vue.component('parent-component', {
  data: function() {
    return {
      message: 'Hello World'
    }
  },
  template: `
    <div>
      <child-component :message="message" @message-updated="
          handleMessageUpdate"></child-component>
    </div>
  `,
```

```
methods: {
  handleMessageUpdate: function(newMessage) {
    this.message = newMessage
  }
}
})
```

In this example, the 'parent-component' is passing a 'message' to the 'child-component' via props. Whenever the 'child-component' needs to update this message, it emits a 'message-updated' event which the 'parent-component' listens for and updates its data accordingly.

The limitation of this approach is that it's really only suitable for direct parent-child component communication.

2. **Provide / Inject**: This method is a more advanced feature in Vue.js, but it can be useful for avoiding prop drilling. The provide / inject API allows you to pass data from a parent component to descendant components (not just direct children) without having to pass props through every level of the component tree (which could be cumbersome and unnecessary).

```
// Parent Component
Vue.component('parent-component', {
  provide: function() {
    return {
      message: 'Hello World'
    }
  }
});

// Descendant Component
Vue.component('descendant-component', {
  inject: ['message'],
  template: '<div>{{ message }}</div>'
});
```

In this example, the descendant component can directly access the 'message' provided by its ancestor component. The advantage of this approach is that it can cover more complex scenarios where components might be more deeply nested. But it also makes your components more tightly coupled and harder to reuse elsewhere in your code because they become more reliant on their parent context.

5.10   Describe the process of writing and distributing a Vue plugin.

Writing and distributing a Vue.js plugin involves several key steps. I'll mention these and then get into more details:

1. Writing the Plugin

2. Bundling the Plugin

3. Publishing the Plugin to NPM

4. Installing and Using the Plugin in a Vue Application

Now let me explain these steps in detail:

1. **Writing the Plugin**: A Vue plugin should expose an 'install' method. The 'install' method will be called with the Vue constructor as the first argument, along with possible options:

```
export default {
  install(Vue, options) {
    // Plugin code goes here
  }
}
```

For example, if you're writing a plugin to add a global method or property, you might write:

```
export default {
  install(Vue, options) {
    Vue.prototype.$myAddedProperty = 'This␣is␣a␣Vue␣plugin';
  }
}
```

The above plugin when installed, will add a new property '$myAdded-Property' to all Vue instances.

2. **Bundling the Plugin**: Once your plugin is written, you'll need to bundle it into a JavaScript file that can be included in a Vue project. We can use module bundlers like Webpack or Rollup for bundling the plugin. The bundling process typically involves transpilation (converting modern JavaScript into code interpreted accurately

by most browsers), minification, etc.

3. **Publishing the Plugin to NPM**: Once the plugin is bundled, you'll want to make it available for other developers to use and contribute to. The most common approach is to publish the plugin to the npm registry. To do this, you'll need to create a package.json file that describes your plugin, and run 'npm publish'. Make sure your package.json contains "main" field which points to the entry point of your plugin. Example package.json:

```
{
  "name": "my-vue-plugin",
  "version": "1.0.0",
  "description": "My Vue.js plugin",
  "main": "dist/my-vue-plugin.js",
  ...
}
```

Run 'npm publish' to publish it to npm registry.

4. **Installing and Using the Plugin in a Vue Application**: The final step is to install and use your plugin in a Vue.js application. Users can install it using NPM or Yarn.

```
npm install my-vue-plugin
```

After that, they need to import it and use in main.js file

```
import Vue from 'vue';
import MyVuePlugin from 'my-vue-plugin';

Vue.use(MyVuePlugin);

new Vue({
  render: h => h(App),
}).$mount('#app')
```

In this way, a Vue developer can write, distribute and use a Vue plugin.

5.11 How do you integrate Vue with non-Vue libraries or legacy systems?

Integrating Vue.js with non-Vue libraries or legacy systems requires careful planning and implementation in order to avoid damaging or rendering the existing system non-functional. Here's how it can be done.

1. **Use Vue.js in Part of the Application:**

Vue.js is a progressive framework. This means that it is designed to be incrementally adoptable. In simpler terms, you can use Vue in just a part of your project without having to implement it throughout the application. This makes it a great fit for integrating with non-Vue libraries or legacy systems to improve part of the project you are working on without affecting the rest of the application.

For example, you could use Vue components in a certain part of your application and still be able to use jQuery or any other library in other parts of the application.

```
// Instantiating Vue in a specific part of the application
new Vue({
  el: '#app'
})
```

In the above example, Vue would only take control of the div with 'id='app''. This allows other libraries to operate effectively in other areas of the application.

2. **Vue Components as Web Components:**

Vue provides "vue-custom-element" package which allows you to use your Vue components as custom HTML elements. This approach is useful if you need to insert Vue functionality into a legacy application where rewriting all coded components into Vue would be excessively laborious or even counter-productive.

```
import Vue from 'vue';
import vueCustomElement from 'vue-custom-element';
```

```
// my-component is your Vue component
import MyComponent from './my-component.vue';

Vue.use(vueCustomElement);
MyComponent.install = function(Vue){
  Vue.component('my-component', MyComponent);
};

const CustomElement = Vue.component('my-component').extend(MyComponent);
customElements.define('my-component', CustomElement);
```

In the above example, a Vue component is exposed as a custom HTML element that can be used throughout the project, regardless of the legacy libraries that the project is based on.

3. **Integration with Server-Side Rendered Applications:**

Vue can be integrated with server-side rendered applications as well. You can mount Vue on specific element on the DOM and use Vue's server-side rendering capabilities to render Vue components on the server and then mount them on the client.

4. **Use Vue as Reactive Library:**

Sometimes, you don't want a full-featured SPA or need to integrate Vue in places where you just need reactivity. Vue can be used simply for its reactivity features, acting like a more convenient replacement for data binding libraries (like Handlebars or Mustache).

Vue's approachable core library focuses on the view layer only, making it easy to pick up and integrate with other libraries or existing projects.

5.12 Discuss strategies for optimizing Vue component re-renders.

When you're developing an application with Vue.js, your goal is often to ensure that components re-render as efficiently as possible to ensure

peak performance. Here are some strategies you can use to optimize
Vue component re-rendering:

1. Use 'v-once': This is a Vue directive that ensures that a component
only renders once and never re-renders. This is great for static content
which doesn't have any reactive data, thus saving the unnecessary
cycles.

Example:

```
<div v-once>{{ staticContent }}</div>
```

2. Use of 'v-show' over 'v-if': 'v-if' is "real" conditional rendering
because it ensures that event listeners and child components inside
the conditional block are properly destroyed and re-created during
toggles. On the other hand, 'v-show' is much simpler - the element is
always rendered regardless of initial condition, with simple switching
of CSS based on the condition. If you need to toggle something very
often, 'v-show' will be more efficient.

3. Use of computed properties: One of the powerful features of Vue.js
is computed properties. Computed properties are like methods but
they only re-run when a piece of data they use changes. This can
optimize re-rendering and data calculation processes.

Example:

```
computed: {
  fullName() {
    return this.firstName + '␣' + this.lastName
  }
}
```

4. Lazy-loading components: Vue allows you to define your component as a factory function that asynchronously resolves your component definition. This is particularly useful when you know certain
components will not be necessary an application. This reduces the
initial load time and optimizes the performance.

Example:

```
Vue.component('async-component', function (resolve, reject) {
  setTimeout(function () {
    // Pass the component definition to the resolve callback
    resolve({
      template: '<div>I am async!</div>'
    })
  }, 1000)
})
```

5. Component key: If you are using 'v-for' directives with components, always use ':key' values. The key helps Vue recognize nodes
when the order has changed and reuses existing elements in a more
efficient way, improving re-rendering.

Example:

```
<my-comp v-for="item in items" :key="item.id"></my-comp>
```

6. Avoid using the '@change' or '@input' event directly in v-model
on components: For each time the component's model changes, this
event is triggered, and thereby Vue re-renders the component. If the
component is complex, this can create serious performance issues.

Remember, optimization is highly dependent on the specific use case,
so while general practices are provided, it's still required to perform
your own benchmarking and testing.

5.13   How do you handle complex form logic and validation in Vue?

Handling complex form logic and validation in Vue.js usually involves
leveraging Vue's inbuilt directives like 'v-model', and some external
libraries like Vuelidate or Vee-Validate. This allows you to maintain
form validation in-line with the Vue's reactive data system.

Here's a step-by-step approach for this process:

Step 1: Create the form template with v-model For instance, a simple form can be modeled as such:

```
<form @submit.prevent="submitForm">
    <input type="text" v-model="formData.name" />
    <input type="email" v-model="formData.email" />
    <button type="submit">Submit</button>
</form>
```

Step 2: Managing the form data The form fields are populated from the 'data' method in Vue instance:

```
data() {
    return {
        formData: {
            name: '',
            email: ''
        }
    };
}
```

Step 3: Validating the form Now to handle complex validations, you can use a library like Vuelidate. First, install it in your project

```
npm install vuelidate
```

Import it in your component:

```
import { required, email } from 'vuelidate/lib/validators'
```

Apply validations in your component:

```
validations: {
    formData: {
        name: { required },
        email: { required, email }
    }
}
```

With Vuelidate, you get access to states like *invalid*, 'dirty' etc., for each field. So, you can use these states to show error messages or disable the submit button.

```
<input type="text" v-model="formData.name" />
<div v-if="$v.formData.name.$dirty && !$v.formData.name.required">Name is
    required</div>

<button :disabled="$v.formData.$invalid" type="submit">Submit</button>
```

Step 4: Submitting the form Finally, on form submission, you can check if the form is valid using '*v.formData*.invalid', and then proceed as per your app's flow:

```
methods: {
    submitForm() {
        this.$v.form.$touch();
        if (this.$v.formData.$invalid) {
            // show some global error message
        } else {
            // process form
        }
    }
}
```

Vuelidate also provides a '*touch*'*methodthatsetsthe*'dirty' state for all fields, which can be useful to enforce validation on form submission.

This is a very basic example. Based on your requirements, the complexity can increase, like handling multiple form sections, validating arrays or complex objects, cross-field validations etc.

5.14   Describe how Vue 3's reactivity system differs from Vue 2, especially with the introduction of Proxies.

In Vue 2, Vue's reactivity system was primarily based on ES5, specifically the Object.defineProperty API. While this API worked well for Vue 2, it had several limitations. For example, it was not capable of detecting when a property was added to or deleted from an object, meaning Vue could not automatically update the UI to reflect these changes.

Vue 2's reactivity system looked like this:

```
let data = { name: 'John' };
let vm = new Vue({
  data
});
```

If you modify the 'name' property, Vue 2 would be able to detect the changes and perform necessary UI updates. However, if you add a new property after the Vue instance has been created, Vue 2 couldn't detect that:

```
vm.$set(data, 'age', 30); // Vue 2
```

In comparison, Vue 3's reactivity system leverages the Proxy API in ES6. Proxies are a powerful tool that allow us to customize fundamental JavaScript operations, such as getting/setting properties, function invocation, etc.

With the Proxy API, Vue 3's reactivity system can now detect when a property is added to or deleted from an object. In addition, Vue 3's reactivity system can also handle arrays naturally and has better performance and memory efficiency.

Here's what creating a reactive object looks like in Vue 3:

```
import { reactive } from 'vue';
let data = reactive({ name: 'John' });
```

Now, Vue 3 can detect when you add a new property:

```
data.age = 30; // Vue 3 can detect this change
```

To summarize, Vue 3's use of the Proxy API allows for much more powerful and efficient reactivity than was possible in Vue 2. However, it's worth noting that because Proxies are not available in Internet Explorer, Vue 3 does not support this browser. Meanwhile, Vue 2 is still available for projects that require Internet Explorer support.

5.15   How do you handle caching strategies in a Vue application?

Caching in a Vue.js application can be addressed in various ways, but here are a few popular methods and tools developers find particularly helpful:

1. **Vue Component Caching with 'v-once':** Vue.js provides an in-built way to cache a component during its initial rendering through the 'v-once' directive. This directive ensures the element and all its child nodes remain as static content after its initial rendering.

```
<div v-once>
  {{ staticContent }}
</div>
```

Here, 'staticContent' will be rendered only once and Vue.js will store and reuse the virtual nodes present in this part of the application.

2. **Computed Properties:** One of the optimal ways to handle caching is by leveraging Vue's 'computed properties'. Computed properties cache their return values until their dependencies change. A computed property will only re-evaluate when some of its reactive dependencies have changed.

```
computed: {
  fullName: function() {
    return this.firstName + ' ' + this.lastName;
  }
}
```

In this example, 'fullName' is a computed property, which depends on 'firstName' and 'lastName'. This computed property will be cached and will not re-evaluate until either 'firstName' or 'lastName' changes.

3. **Vue-Apollo and GraphQL:** Vue-Apollo is a Vue.js integration for Apollo, which uses GraphQL for data management. Apollo Client comes packaged with an intelligent cache which automatically caches query results. This helps you to avoid making identical queries to your backend.

4. **Server-side Caching:** Vue Server Renderer provides the options to cache rendered components using a LRU cache out-of-the-box. When using server-side rendering (SSR) with 'vue-server-renderer', the application can take advantage of component-level caching to cache the parts of the application that do not change and serve these

parts from the cache.

5. **Service Worker and Progressive Web Apps (PWA):** PWAs
with Vue.js are usually built using plugins like 'vue-pwa', which can
be used to handle caching strategies by leveraging Service Workers.
Service Workers can cache static files, API responses, and other data.

Remember, each strategy has its own trade-offs, and every project
may require a strategy that best matches its unique requirements.
Hence, it's essential to find an optimal balance to effectively use
caching mechanisms.

5.16   Discuss the best practices for ensuring accessibility (A11y) in Vue applications.

Ensuring accessibility is vital in any application, and Vue.js is no
different. By following certain best practices, one can make their
Vue applications more accessible (A11y) to a wider range of users,
including those with disabilities.

1. **Use Semantic HTML**: This is the basis of any accessible web
application. Screen readers and other assistive technologies rely on
understanding the intent of elements through their semantic tags, so
it's important to use the correct tags wherever possible.

2. **Manage Focus**: You should ensure that your application can
be used without a pointer device. This usually involves ensuring that
all interactive elements are focusable and that the focus order makes
sense. Vue.js does not automatically shift focus when a route changes,
so you have to manually set the focus each time. You can do this with
'this.$refs.element.focus()'.

```
// Setting focus in mounted hook
export default {
  mounted() {
    this.$refs.element.focus();
```

```
    }
  }
```

3. **Provide Text Alternatives**: All non-text content such as images should have text alternatives that serve the equivalent purpose. Using 'v-bind', you can bind the 'alt' attribute to the image's data.

```
// Using v-bind for alt text
<img v-bind:src="imageSrc" v-bind:alt="imageAltText">
```

4. **Use ARIA Attributes**: ARIA (Accessible Rich Internet Applications) attributes help to improve the accessibility of your Vue.js application by providing extra information to assistive technology. Vue.js supports binding to these attributes out of the box.

```
// Using ARIA attributes
<button v-bind:aria-expanded="isExpanded">Toggle</button>
```

5. **Use Keyboard Accessible Custom Inputs**: Ensure that custom inputs created can be tabbed to, focused on and interacted with ensuring keyboard navigation.

6. **Use Vue CLI's Accessibility Plugin**: Using this plugin, you can perform accessibility auditing using AXE and get realtime feedback on violations as you code.

7. **Testing**: Make sure to test your application with actual assistive technology like a screen reader. Automated testing tools can also be very helpful here.

8. **Avoid using 'v-html' for user-generated content**: This can lead to Cross-Site Scripting (XSS) attacks, where hackers inject malicious scripts. Instead, use only for trusted content and consider alternatives, such as 'v-text'.

By incorporating these best practices, developers can ensure that their Vue.js applications are accessible to all users, regardless of their abilities or disabilities.

5.17   How would you implement end-to-end testing in a Vue application?

End-to-end testing in a Vue.js application can be implemented using several testing tools like Cypress, TestCafe, Nightwatch.js, etc. Here, I will describe the steps using Cypress, an end-to-end testing framework that makes it easy to set up, write, run, and debug tests.

Step 1: Installation of Cypress To begin, you need to install Cypress. In your project directory run the following command.

```
npm install cypress --save-dev
```

Step 2: Setting up test files Cypress will create a 'cypress' directory at the base of your project. This directory stores all your tests and Cypress configuration. A typical Cypress test file may look like this:

```
describe('My First Test', () => {
  it('Does not do much!', () => {
    expect(true).to.equal(true)
  })
})
```

Step 3: Writing Tests With a Vue.js application, you're generally testing the final output, the DOM. You can use Cypress commands like 'cy.visit()', 'cy.get()', 'cy.click()', etc. to interact with your application. For example, to test a login functionality, you'll write:

```
describe('The Login Page', () => {
  it('successfully logs in', () => {
    cy.visit('/login') // Goes to the login URL
    cy.get('input[name=username]').type('myusername') // Types in the username
    cy.get('input[name=password]').type('mypassword') // Types in the password
    cy.get('button[type=submit]').click() // Clicks the submit button
    // Now, it checks if it successfully logged in by asserting the presence of
    //    the logout button
    cy.get('button[name=logout]').should('be.visible')
  })
})
```

Step 4: Running tests You can run Cypress tests using the following command:

```
npx cypress open
```

This will open the Cypress Test Runner. You can then select the specific test file you want to run, and Cypress will execute the tests.

For best practices with E2E testing in Vue.js, always make sure you have a clear understanding of the user flows you intend to test. Start by writing E2E tests for critical user journeys like logging in, signing up, etc. For further testing, unit tests and integration tests would be more beneficial.

It's also helpful that you run your E2E tests on every commit to prevent regressions and ensure that any breaking changes are caught immediately. This can be achieved through Continuous Integration (CI) tools like CircleCI or Jenkins.

5.18 Describe the challenges of migrating a large-scale Vue 2 application to Vue 3.

Migrating a large-scale Vue 2 application to Vue 3 can present several challenges, some of which include:

1. **Breaking changes**: Every new version of a library or framework brings about some breaking changes, and Vue 3 is no different. For instance, with Vue 3, Vue.set and Vue.delete have been removed from the API as they are no longer necessary due to Vue 3's new reactivity system powered by ES6 Proxy. Thus, this breaking change would mean developers will have to rework parts of their codes that use Vue.set and Vue.delete.

2. **Architecture changes (Composition API) & Modularity**: Vue 3 introduces a new API for managing component logic called the Composition API. While the Options API from Vue 2.x is still available and not going anywhere, using the Composition API can lead

to better logic organization and code reuse. However, refactoring an existing Vue 2.x application to use the Composition API can be challenging and time-consuming due to the large-scale changes to how the codebase is structured. Some plugins/modules might not work as expected when working with the Composition API.

3. **Updating third-party packages**: If your Vue 2 application uses third-party libraries, plugins, or projects, you may face challenges updating these to be compatible with Vue 3. You'll have to ensure that each library you choose is fully compatible or has a Vue 3 equivalent to avoid breaking your application.

4. **V-model changes**: In Vue 2, v-model was used for two-way data binding on every component. But in Vue 3, the v-model syntax has changed, and this might result in issues in case there are many components with v-model being used, since each of them would require manual correction.

5. **Vue Router and Vuex**: Vue Router and Vuex have their version released which will be compatible with Vue 3. Therefore, using them in their previous versions might not be compatible and this requires a good amount of time to migrate.

6. **Size of the application**: In a large-scale application, even a small change can affect many different parts of the application, making it harder and more time-consuming to migrate and test.

7. **Learning curve**: Front End developers familiar with Vue 2 will need to learn and understand the new features and changes in Vue 3, including the Composition API, before they can be productive in migrating a Vue 2 application.

8. **Testing and Debugging**: After migration, thorough testing of the applications is needed to ensure all features are working properly. Debugging to find hidden bugs which may come due to migration is also an issue. Tools used in Vue 2.x for debugging might not work as expected with Vue 3.

For every challenge involved in the migration, it is advised to plan the

migration and to not rush to adopt any new version before making
sure it is stable and actually offers the benefits it promises.

5.19 How do you handle state synchronization between server and client in a Vue application?

Synchronization of state between server and client in a Vue.js application can be efficiently handled through the Vue.js component ecosystem. This system is composed of parent components, root instances, and child components. When an event occurs in a child component which requires a state change, this child component will not directly modify its own state or the state of the parent component. Instead, it will signal the event to the parent component or root instance.

However, managing state between server and client in Vue.js applications can get complex as the application grows larger. Larger applications may have multiple components that share and manipulate the same state. This is where VueX comes into play. VueX is a state management library specifically developed to work with Vue.js.

In Vuex, the state of your Vue application is stored in a centralized and observable store, and any state-modifying operations are done in a predictable way. Vuex provides a single source of truth for your application state, making it possible to track state changes over time, easily understand how and when state changes occurred, and ensuring that state changes are consistently applied.

A typical Vuex flow works like this:

1) Components dispatch an action.

2) Actions commit mutations.

3) Mutations change the state.

4) The state change triggers a re-render of components.

Example Vuex code:

```
new Vuex.Store({
    // The state object
    state: {
      count: 0
    },
    // The mutations object
    mutations: {
      increment (state) {
        state.count++
      }
    },
    // The actions object
    actions: {
      increment (context) {
        context.commit('increment')
      }
    },
})
```

In your Vue component, you would then map Vuex state and actions:

```
import { mapState, mapActions } from 'vuex'

export default {
  // computed property for mapping state
  computed: mapState([
    'count'
  ]),
  methods: {
    // mapping actions
    ...mapActions([
      'increment'
    ])
  }
}
```

When it comes to actual data synchronization between client and server, Vue.js does not have its own out-of-the-box solution. However, integration with libraries such as axios or fetch API is often used to handle HTTP requests to perform actual server-client synchronization.

Axios, for instance, can be used in Vuex action to trigger a state change:

```
actions: {
  increment (context) {
    axios.get('/api/data')
      .then(response => context.commit('increment', response.data));
  }
```

```
}
```

In this case, the 'increment' mutation will also take a second argument, which is the server response data. This way, Vuex controls not only the local state of the Vue.js components but also the state synchronization between client and server.

5.20 Discuss strategies for implementing micro-frontends using Vue.

Micro-frontend is a design approach in which a front-end app is decomposed into "micro" independent parts which can be developed and deployed independently. This approach is beneficial in terms of code base organization, individual team autonomy, and technology flexibility.

When we talk about Vue.js, there are several strategies to implement micro-frontends, among these are:

1. **Iframes**: One of the most basic approaches, you can include different Vue applications in iframes. This would allow each of them to function in their own realm, without conflicts. However, communication between different Vue applications could be a bit complex, as iframe content is isolated from the parent page.

2. **Web Components**: One modern approach could be leveraging the Web Components standard (Custom Elements, Shadow DOM, etc.). Each Vue app could be encapsulated in a custom element, keeping its own styles and behaviors without affecting others.

3. **Single-spa**: A Javascript framework that allows you to build micro-frontends. With single-spa, you would have a root application and multiple child applications (which can be Vue apps). Each of these child applications can be loaded, unmounted, mounted, and communicate with each other independently. This way, you can use

Vue.js in some parts of your frontend while using other frameworks in other parts without any conflict.

Here is an example of using single-spa for Vue:

```
import Vue from 'vue';
import singleSpaVue from 'single-spa-vue';
import HelloWorld from './main.vue';

const vueLifecycles = singleSpaVue({
Vue,
appOptions: {
    el: '#vue-app',
    render: (r) => r(HelloWorld),
    }
});

export const bootstrap = [vueLifecycles.bootstrap];
export const mount = [vueLifecycles.mount];
export const unmount = [vueLifecycles.unmount];
```

4. **Vue CLI 3.0 and higher Instant Prototyping + Micro-Frontend Structure**: Vue CLI 3.0 introduced a new feature called Instant Prototyping. You can rapidly prototype an application without any boilerplate considerations. Every Micro-frontend can be a prototype, distributed on a CDN, and work as an autonomous entity.

5. **Micro-APP**: This is another approach, originally proposed developed by the Chinese company, Meituan. The 'Micro-APP' provides a similar isolation experience to iframes, but they all exist in the same DOM tree with Shadow DOM providing the required isolation.

Note: While this approach may provide a lot of flexibility, it can bring complexity, make sure your project complexity justifies this architectural choice. Also, it's very important to have shared components to avoid duplication and inconsistencies and have a detailed documentation for easy navigation within the code and modules. Maintain a balance between the autonomy granted to individual teams and the overall cohesiveness of the user experience.

Remember, the micro-frontend approach is not for all applications. Each architecture has its own pros and cons, and as a developer we have to understand the needs and requirements clearly before we decide the architecture of the application. Micro-frontends are best suited to large-scale applications with multiple teams working in parallel.

Chapter 6

Master

6.1 Discuss the internal architecture of Vue.js. How are the core modules structured?

Vue.js is a progressive JavaScript framework used to create interactive web interfaces. It's a modular framework that offers a simple way to manage complex UI state and provides a high-performance, reactive system for updating the DOM.

The Vue.js architecture is divided into several core modules, each responsible for a specific functionality. Let's discuss these in detail:

1. **Observer:** This is the reactive data model of Vue.js. It uses the ES5 Object.defineProperty API to convert regular JavaScript objects into reactive objects. Whenever a property of this object changes, the system is notified.

2. **Virtual DOM:** Similar to other popular frameworks like ReactJS, Vue.js uses a Virtual DOM to make changes to the web page more efficient. Instead of directly manipulating the DOM every time

a change is made, Vue creates a lightweight copy of the real DOM (Virtual DOM), and whenever a change is made, it updates this Virtual DOM first.

3. **Compiler:** It compiles the templates into Virtual DOM render functions. In the process of compiling, it also detects certain directives (if present) like v-if, v-for, v-on, etc and does special handling for them.

4. **Watcher:** Vue.js provides the ability to watch for data changes. When a component's data changes, the watcher triggers a rerender of the component's template.

5. **Scheduler:** This module is responsible for assessing dependencies, and managing and queuing watchers so that each watcher runs only once in every tick. This is also where Vue's asynchrony and nextTick method play a central role.

6. **Dep:** It is a simple class that serves as the dependency tracking mechanism. Essentially, it is an array of all the Watchers that depend on a reactive property. When a property changes, the Dep class notifies all of its subscribers (Watchers).

Here's how they all work together:

1. Vue components templates are passed to the compiler.

2. The Compiler compiles the templates into a render function that produces a Virtual DOM tree.

3. The render function is observed by the Observer.

4. When the state changes, the render function is run again, producing a new Virtual DOM tree.

5. The new Virtual DOM tree is compared to the old one by the scheduler. The differences are calculated and a list of patches (changes) is produced.

6. These patches are used to update the actual DOM.

This structure helps in creating an efficient, reactive system with updates that are deterministic, minimal, and optimized out of the box. The division into different modules helps Vue to be progressive and flexible, as developers can choose to use only some of the modules or use them all together for more complex applications.

6.2 How would you design a real-time collaborative application using Vue? Discuss potential challenges and solutions.

Designing a real-time collaborative application using Vue.js would involve connecting Vue.js to a real-time backend such as WebSockets or Firebase. The general architecture would involve Vue.js for the front end and the real-time backend handling the data synchronization requirements.

Here's a general process to follow:

1. **Vue Component Design:** Start by identifying the different components of your application. In Vue, it's recommended to build your user interface into components where each component has its own HTML, CSS, and JavaScript needed to power it. For example, in a collaborative text editor app, you might have components such as 'Editor', 'UserList', 'RevisionHistory', etc.

2. **Real-time backend integration:** Vue.js integrates well with various real-time backend solutions. One such popular choice is Firebase, which provides real-time database features. Alternatively, you could use WebSockets. Understanding how to emit and listen to events is key to implementing real-time features. For example, you might emit events whenever a user updates the shared document, and listen for those events on all clients so they can update their views of the document.

3. **VueX/Store for state management:** Vuex is the state management solution for Vue.js. In a real-time collaborative application, maintaining and syncing the state across all clients can be challeng-

ing. Vuex can be helpful in managing the state of the application in a centralized way.

Potential Challenges and Solutions:

1. Consistency: Ensuring that all users are viewing the latest and consistent data is a common challenge in real-time collaborative applications. This can be handled by syncing any changes to the data made by a user immediately to the central server which then pushes these changes to all other users.

2. Collision of updates: Another issue occurs when two or more users try to update the same piece of data simultaneously. This can be handled with Oplocks (Optimistic Locking) where the "lock" is a version, and before committing the operation, the version is verified. If it's outdated, an error is returned.

3. Latency: Latency can be a problem, particularly in applications featuring many real-time updates. This can cause slow performance and a less responsive user interface. To handle this, use efficient data structures and algorithms, minimize the amount of data sent over the network, and consider giving users visual feedback to indicate that updates are in progress.

4. Security and access control: Managing who can and cannot access certain data or operations is another challenge. Firebase and similar solutions offer built-in access control mechanisms that allow you to easily specify who can access what data and when.

Here's a sample code snippet demonstrating how you might implement real-time updates with Vue and Firebase:

```
import { ref, onUnmounted } from 'vue'
import { db } from './firebase'

const useDocument = (collection, id) => {
  const error = ref(null)
  const isPending = ref(null)

  let docRef = db.collection(collection).doc(id)
  const unsubscribe = docRef.onSnapshot(doc => {
    // update the application state with real-time changes
  }, err => {
```

```
    console.log(err.message)
    isPending.value = false
    error.value = 'could␣not␣fetch␣the␣data'
  })

  onUnmounted(unsubscribe)

  return { error, isPending }
}

export default useDocument
```

In this example, 'useDocument' is a custom Hook that starts listening to real-time updates from Firestore when the component that uses this Hook is mounted to the DOM, and stops listening when the component is unmounted. This helps ensure that your application's state always reflects the latest updates from your Firestore database.

6.3 Describe the trade-offs between using Vue's reactivity system and other reactive programming paradigms, like RxJS.

Vue's reactivity system and other reactive programming paradigms, like RxJS, offer different trade-offs based on factors which include learning curve, complexity, control and suitability for specific use-cases.

1. Learning Curve: Vue's reactive system is relatively easy to understand and use. It is also well integrated with Vue's ecosystem and does not require the learning of additional libraries or concepts. On the other hand, reactive programming libraries like RxJS have a steep learning curve and many complex concepts and operators are difficult to grasp for beginners.

2. Complexity: The complexity of Vue's reactivity system is fairly low, you can achieve a lot of functionality with its straightforward programming model. Conversely, RxJS allows you to express complex

data transformation and manipulation scenarios. This complexity, however, can often lead to harder-to-read or harder-to-maintain code if not well-structured or if the developer is not well-versed in reactive programming concepts.

3. Control: RxJS provides more fine-grained control as compared to Vue's reactive system. It allows for complex composition of asynchronous operations, advanced error handling, and fine control over resource handling and timing. Vue's reactive system, however, is more automatic and doesn't provide the same level of control.

4. Suitability: Vue's reactivity system is more suitable for straightforward, component-based UI updates. For applications with highly complex state management requirements, combining Vue's reactivity system with Vuex (Vue's own state-management library) is often a good choice. RxJS, on the other hand, is more suitable for applications with complex asynchronous data flow or those that need to maintain a high level of control over the data flow.

In terms of integration, Vue and RxJS can be used together. Vue-Rx is a library that allows Vue's reactivity system and RxJS to be combined, making it possible to take advantage of the strengths of both. However, it would definitely increase the complexity of the codebase and is generally recommended for developers who are comfortable with both Vue.js and RxJS concepts.

6.4   How would you handle versioning and backward compatibility when developing and maintaining a Vue plugin or library?

Developing and maintaining a Vue.js plugin or library involves careful consideration of versioning and backward compatibility. Here is how to handle these aspects:

1. **Semantic Versioning**: This is a crucial aspect of version management. Take advantage of the semantic versioning (SemVer) system. The versioning follows the format 'MAJOR.MINOR.PATCH'. Here a 'MAJOR' version indicates incompatible API changes, 'MINOR' version indicates that a new functionality is added in a backwards-compatible manner, and 'PATCH' version means that backwards-compatible bug fixes were introduced.

2. **Document Changes**: Make sure all changes in the versions are comprehensively documented. The documentation should show exactly which features were added, modified, or removed in each version. If breaking changes are introduced, they should be clearly outlined and instructions given on how to migrate to the new version.

3. **Testing**: Carry out extensive testing before releasing a new version. Unit testing, integration testing, and regression testing are crucial to ensure that the new version is stable and all older features are still compatible.

4. **Deprecation Strategy**: If there are any changes that will break backward compatibility, consider a deprecation strategy instead of sudden removal. Deprecation warnings can be used to let the users know that certain features are about to be removed in future releases. This also gives them time to adjust their code.

5. **Maintaining Older Versions**: While not always possible or practical, in some cases you might need to maintain older versions of your plugin/library for a while even after releasing new major versions. This could mean fixing critical bugs or security vulnerabilities on these older versions.

6. **Release Notes**: Always create release notes with each new version. These notes should contain detailed information about new implementations and alterations if any. It should also indicate the changes impacting the previous version and the measures taken for backward compatibility.

For example, consider a Vue plugin 'MyPlugin':

```
// @ v1.0.0
new Vue({
  methods: {
    initialize() {
      // Initial setup code
    }
  }
});
```

If in version '2.0.0' you decide to replace the method 'initialize' with 'start', you could keep backward compatibility intact by deprecating 'initialize' instead of suddenly removing it:

```
// @ v2.0.0
new Vue({
  methods: {
    initialize() {
      console.warn('initialize is deprecated, please use start.');
      this.start();
    },
    start() {
      // Initial setup code
    }
  }
});
```

This will ensure that applications using 'initialize' will still work, but developers will be warned about the deprecation and suggested to switch to the new method 'start'.

6.5 Discuss the potential pitfalls of Vue's reactivity system when working with native JavaScript data structures like Maps and Sets.

Vue.js provides a reactivity system that is highly efficient and flexible. It tracks all the dependencies of a reactive property during its render, so when the property changes, all the related widgets will re-render immediately.

However, there are some limitations when Vue's reactivity system works with native JavaScript data structures like Maps and Sets.

Vue cannot detect the following changes to an array or an object:

1. When you directly set an item with the index, example: 'vm.arr[index] = newValue'

2. When you modify the length of the array, example: 'vm.arr.length = newLength'

3. Adding new properties to an object after it has been created, you should use 'Vue.set(object, key, value)' or 'vm.$set(vm.user, 'newProp', 'newValue')'

4. Deleting properties from an object, you should use 'Vue.delete(object, key)' or 'vm.$delete(vm.user, 'oldProp')'

And for Map and Set, Vue does not have build-in reactivity, so any changes made to these types would not be picked up by Vue's reactivity system. For example, if you initialize a Vue data property with a Set or a Map:

```
data: function() {
  return {
    mySet: new Set([1, 2, 3]),
    myMap: new Map([['key', 'value']])
  }
}
```

You can modify 'mySet' and 'myMap' as you wish, but Vue.js won't pick up these changes and won't cause the component to update.

In order to observe changes in these data structures, a simple solution like converting them to arrays or objects before modifying them can be adopted. Or the later version Vue3 has solved the reactivity for Map and Set with its Proxy-based reactivity system.

6.6   How would you optimize a Vue application for a low-memory environment?

Optimizing a Vue.js application for a low-memory environment involves multiple techniques and best practices that developers can follow. Here are some of them:

1. **Code-Splitting or Lazy Loading**: A fundamental strategy to reduce the memory footprint of a Vue.js application is to use code-splitting or lazy-loading to reduce the size of the initial JavaScript payload that is sent to the client. This can be achieved by using the dynamic 'import()' syntax in your routes definition.

For example:

```
const Foo = () => import('./Foo.vue')
```

This creates a separate chunk for 'Foo.vue' and its dependencies, which will only be requested when the route is visited.

2. **Optimized Build**: Use webpack's 'optimization.splitChunks' options to create common chunks of the code which can be shared across multiple bundles.

3. **Avoiding Global Component Registration**. Instead of globally registering all components, developers can register components locally. Thus, components that are not in use do not consume memory.

4. **Using functional components**: Functional components do not have reactivity, lifecycles or internal state. As a result, they consume less memory and render quicker than stateful components.

5. **Good practices with v-for directives**: It's always a good idea to use 'key' when using 'v-for' directive, especially when list data can change. This helps Vue in being more efficient at re-rendering the

list.

6. **Disposing unused components/instances**: Always remember to dispose of components that aren't in use. Vue.js has a '$destroy' method, which can be used to manually release a component.

7. **Efficient use of JavaScript libraries**: JavaScript libraries could consume large amounts of memory. If possible, consider removing them from your dependencies, or replacing them with lighter alternatives.

8. **Performance Monitoring & Profiling**: Tools like the Vue.js devtools can be quite helpful in diagnosing memory issues. It's also a good idea to monitor your application's performance in real-time, using tools like Google Lighthouse or Chrome's performance panel.

9. **Avoiding Memory Leaks**: Always be cautious of potential memory leaks. For example, always clear timers or cancel requests in the 'beforeDestroy' lifecycle method, remove event listeners that are not needed anymore, and carefully use closures, all to ensure you're not retaining memory unnecessarily.

10. **Optimized Images**: Use optimized and properly sized images as large sized images can consume a lot of memory.

These steps, if properly followed, can make a huge difference in memory footprint and the overall performance of a Vue.js application in a low-memory environment.

6.7 Describe the process of integrating Vue with Web Workers or Service Workers.

Web Workers and Service Workers are two powerful tools that would allow a Vue.js application to leverage background processing and

enable functions such as caching and content fetching. Integrating
Vue.js with these workers can bring numerous benefits, including improved performance and a better user experience.

Web Workers run scripts in the background. They don't have any
access to the Document Object Model (DOM). They are mostly used
for tasks that consume a lot of computational power.

Service Workers, a type of Web Worker, emphasize offline-first web
application development. It serves as a network proxy in the web
browser to manage the web/HTTP requests programmatically. The
Service Workers lie between the network and device storage to deliver
the user your app.

Integrating Vue.js with Web Workers:

1. First, you would need to create a worker file. For instance:

```
// MyWebWorker.js
onmessage = function(e) {
  console.log('Web Worker received message:', e.data);
  postMessage('This is the response ' + e.data);
};
```

2. You can then create the worker in your Vue component, send it a
message, and listen to messages from it:

```
import MyWebWorker from 'worker-loader!./MyWebWorker';

export default {
  created() {
    this.worker = new MyWebWorker();

    this.worker.postMessage('Hello, Worker!');

    this.worker.onmessage = (message) => {
      console.log('Message from Web Worker:', message.data);
    };
  }
}
```

3. Also, remember to terminate the 'worker' when the component is
destroyed.

```
destroyed() {
    this.worker.terminate()
```

```
}
```

Integrating Vue.js with Service Workers:

1. We'll start with creating a service-worker.js file:

```
// ServiceWorker.js
self.addEventListener('fetch', function(event) {
  event.respondWith(caches.match(event.request).then(function(response) {

    // Cache-hit
    if (response) {
      return response;
    }

    return fetch(event.request);
  }));
});
```

2. Then, register service worker in your Vue code, preferably in the application's entry point:

```
if ('serviceWorker' in navigator) {
  navigator.serviceWorker.register('./service-worker.js').then((registration)
      => {
    console.log('Service Worker registered with scope:', registration.scope);
  }).catch((error) => {
    console.log('Service Worker registration failed:', error);
  });
}
```

You can use libraries such as Workbox for making the ServiceWorker configuration a bit easier.

Note: Both Web Workers and Service Workers are not exclusive to Vue.js and can be used in any JavaScript framework.

Remember not all webpage features can be made available offline with Service Workers and that not all browsers support Web Workers or Service Workers. Always make sure the application can still function without them.

6.8 How would you implement a custom renderer in Vue, similar to Vue Native or Vue 3's custom renderer API?

In Vue.js there exists a concept of custom renderers which allows you to take the declarative Vue component tree and turn it into instructions for any "backend" of your choice. An example which we can easily see is the Vue Native which is a wrapper around React Native APIs.

In Vue 3, there is an architecture that is designed from the ground-up to be adaptable for different rendering targets. There is now a public API for writing custom renderers for Vue. This means the same Vue component code can be easily adapted for rendering to different targets by switching renderers.

Here are the steps to implement a custom renderer:

1. Install the necessary Vue packages:

```
yarn add @vue/runtime-core
yarn add @vue/reactivity
```

2. Write a custom renderer. The central part of a Vue custom renderer is the 'createRenderer' function from '@vue/runtime-core'. This function takes an options object that provides node operations for the renderer.

```
import { createRenderer } from '@vue/runtime-core'

const { createApp } = createRenderer({

    // Called when a VNode has been mounted or patched
    patchProp(el, key, prevValue, nextValue) {
        if (key === 'on') {
            // special handling for event listeners
            // nextValue is the new event handlers
            // prevValue is the old event handlers
        }
        else {
            // Normal prop, assign it to the element
            el[key] = nextValue
        }
    },
```

```
// create element instance
createElement(tag) {
    return document.createElement(tag)
},

// create text node
createText(text) {
    return document.createTextNode(text)
},

// create comment node
createComment(text) {
    return document.createComment(text)
},

// inserting elements
insert(child, parent, anchor) {
    parent.insertBefore(child, anchor || null)
},

// removing elements
remove(el) {
    const parent = el.parentNode
    if (parent) {
        parent.removeChild(el)
    }
}
})

export default createApp
```

3. Define component and mount it. This uses our custom renderer to create an app and mount a component.

```
import { ref } from '@vue/reactivity'
import createApp from './customRenderer'

const App = {
    setup() {
        const count = ref(0)
        return { count }
    },

    render(ctx) {
        return { /* render implementation */ }
    }
}

createApp(App).mount()
```

The above example is a very simple custom renderer. In reality, custom renderers can get quite complex, especially depending on what your target render platform looks like.

Note: The patchProp method is where a lot of the complex work typically happens. It's responsible for diffing the old and new VNode and applying updates to the actual rendered element. It needs to handle edge cases such as boolean attributes, class bindings, style bindings, event listener binding and unbinding, etc.

6.9 Discuss strategies for server-side rendering (SSR) in high-traffic applications using Vue.

Server Side Rendering (SSR) is useful for improving the initial load time of Vue applications and making them more SEO-friendly. It allows a page to be fully rendered on the server before it is sent to the client-side. This approach is critical for high-traffic applications because it ensures they are quickly available to users without any heavy client-side rendering bottlenecks. Here are a few strategies:

1. **Use of 'vue-server-renderer'**

Vue.js provides an out-of-the-box solution for server-side rendering in the form of 'vue-server-renderer'. It is designed to be used in a Node.js server environment and takes a Vue component as an input and outputs the HTML string.

Example:

```
const createApp = require('./app');
const renderer = require('vue-server-renderer').createRenderer();

const context = { ... };
renderer.renderToString(createApp(context), (err, html) => {
  console.error(err);
  console.log(html);
});
```

2. **Caching**

In high-traffic Vue.js applications, we can improve SSR performance by caching the components' render functions. Two methods can be used to cache components in SSR mode: component-level caching and page-level caching.

- **Component-level caching:** Vue-server-renderer supports component-level caching using its built-in LRU cache or a custom cache. 'vue-server-renderer' comes with a caching mechanism backed by 'lru-cache'. For most apps, this should be enough.

Example:

```
const renderer = require('vue-server-renderer').createRenderer({
  runInNewContext: false,
  cache: require('lru-cache')({
    max: 1000,
    maxAge: 1000 * 60 * 15
  })
});
```

- **Page-level caching:** For pages that rarely change, full-page caching can be implemented employing reverse proxy servers such as Nginx or server-side caching libraries like Varnish.

3. **Pre-fetching and State Management**

In SSR, the application's data needs to be pre-fetched on the server before rendering. Vue.js makes it possible using Vuex in the library's core library for managing states.

Vuex Action is dispatched from the special 'asyncData' lifecycle hook to pre-fetch data and is then stored in a Vuex Store. This technique can prevent additional client-side requests and ensure that the Vue application has complete data before it's rendered.

4. **Streaming**

Vue-server-renderer package supports rendering to a Node.js stream via 'renderer.renderToStream()'. This means we can stream the generated HTML to the client faster without waiting for the whole rendering to finish.

5. **Bundle Renderer**

Vue provides a bundle renderer that pre-compiles the entire application into a JavaScript bundle server-side, then runs this bundle server-side before sending the response to clients. It provides better maintainability and performance.

6. **Scaling**:

Lastly, to handle traffic spikes and have a more stable service, it might be necessary to scale our server-side rendering service. This can be achieved either by vertical scaling (increasing server resources) or horizontal scaling (adding more servers).

Considering all these strategies, it's important to balance between SEO requirements and the server's computational overhead during designing server rendered Vue.js applications.

6.10 How would you handle complex state synchronization across multiple Vue applications or micro-frontends?

Handling complex state synchronization across multiple Vue applications or micro-frontends can be achieved by using a state management pattern/library such as Vuex.

Vuex is a state management library developed specifically for Vue.js. It provides a centralized store for all the components in an application, with rules ensuring that the state can only be mutated in a predictable fashion. Vuex also integrates with Vue's official devtools extension, providing features like time-travel debugging and state snapshot export/import. Here is a basic example of how to use it:

```
// First, install Vuex using either npm or yarn
// then import Vue and Vuex
import Vue from 'vue'
import Vuex from 'vuex'

Vue.use(Vuex)
```

```
// Define your store
const store = new Vuex.Store({
  state: {
    count: 0
  },
  mutations: {
    increment (state) {
      state.count++
    }
  }
})

// To call a mutation, you can call store.commit
store.commit('increment')

console.log(store.state.count) // -> 1
```

While Vuex can be used to manage local state within an application, for synchronizing state across multiple applications (micro-frontends), you can consider using a shared external state store, and subscribing to changes from each micro-frontend. This is useful since each Vue application or micro-frontend would have its own private Vuex store, and would need a way to communicate with the others.

One possible solution is to use a Pub/Sub model with an Observable pattern (e.g. using a library like RxJS). Here, an event bus (or similar mechanism) can be used to publish changes to the shared state, and each micro-frontend would subscribe to these changes and update their own state as necessary.

Also, you can go with more integrated and fully-featured state management solutions like Redux or MobX, which can be used with Vue.Js via wrapper libraries such as vuex-redux, etc. These libraries provide more robust facilities for managing and synchronizing state across complex frontend architectures.

However, for most common state synchronization tasks, Vuex should be perfectly adequate. Its simplicity and tight integration with Vue.js make it an excellent choice for Vue applications at various scales.

6.11 Describe the challenges and solutions for implementing a custom reactivity system in Vue 3 using the lower-level reactivity APIs.

The reactivity system in Vue 3 is a new feature that lets developers manually manage reactivity in their applications. This is a powerful tool, but it also introduces challenges. These include properly updating state, maintaining application performance, avoiding memory leaks, and preserving encapsulation and component reusability.

Here are some specific issues associated with implementing a custom reactivity system and their potential solutions:

1. **Updating State:** One problem is to ensure that all dependencies correctly update whenever a reactive value changes. Without proper care, components could fall out of sync with the application state. Vue 3 introduces a 'reactive()' function that takes an object and returns a reactive proxy of the original. This new object is reactive, meaning changes to its properties will trigger updates to any computed properties or watchers that depend on it.

```
import { reactive } from 'vue'
const state = reactive({
  count: 0
})
```

2. **Application Performance:** Rendering also needs to be as efficient as possible. Vue 3 provides a 'computed()' function which computes a value based on reactive state and caches it. This means that if no reactive dependencies have changed, subsequent reading of a computed property will return the cached value instead of re-evaluating the function.

```
import { reactive, computed } from 'vue'
const state = reactive({
  count: 0
})
const countPlusOne = computed(() => state.count + 1)
```

3. **Avoiding Memory Leaks:** Vue 3 also provide APIs to avoid memory leak: 'onMounted' and 'onUnmounted'. These hooks can be used to set up and tear down reactivity when a component mounts or unmounts, preventing lingering watchers from continuing to update.

```
import { onUnmounted} from 'vue'
onUnmounted(() => {
  // cleanup work
})
```

4. **Preserving encapsulation and component reusability:** To maintain component reusability, you can use 'provide' and 'inject' to pass the reactive object from parent components to child components. This will avoid the props drilling issue and keep your component hierarchy more maintainable.

```
import { provide, inject } from 'vue'

// In parent component
const state = reactive({ count: 0 })
provide('state', state)

// In child component
const state = inject('state')
```

While this does reduce platform overhead and provide more flexibility, one downside is that developers must now manage these concerns directly. However, these new APIs also enable more powerful component patterns, such as the new Composition API, that make it easier to deal with larger, more complex state management situations.

6.12 How would you approach optimizing a Vue application for a Content Delivery Network (CDN)?

There are several ways to leverage a Content Delivery Network (CDN) to optimize a Vue.js application. Primarily, you would want to focus on implementing strategies to reduce load times, improve asset delivery, and enhance user experience. Here are some ways you could approach this:

1. **Serve Static Assets via CDN**: Your application's static files such as JavaScript, CSS, fonts, and images can be served via a CDN. For Vue.js, after you build your application using the build command ('yarn build' or 'npm run build'), you can upload the content of the 'dist' directory (contains bundled and minified files) to your CDN. You can automate this process by integrating it into your CI/CD pipeline.

Example:

```
module.exports = {
  // ...
  assetsPublicPath: 'https://mycdn.com/myapp/'
  // ...
}
```

2. **Use CDN for Libraries**: Most likely your Vue.js application is using some external libraries such as Vue Router, Vuex, Axios, or others. You should load these libraries from a CDN if possible, since often users will already have these popular libraries cached in their browser from other sites that used the same CDN.

3. **Use HTTP/2**: Modern CDNs support HTTP/2, which eliminates the need for domain sharding and allows multiplexing, reducing the amount of data that needs to be transferred.

4. **Caching**: Make use of caching through your CDN. You want to ensure that you properly set the cache control headers for your assets so that they are not re-downloaded unnecessarily.

5. **Enable compression**: Many CDNs offer automatic gzip or Brotli compression for files that they serve. Enabling compression makes your files smaller and faster to download.

6. **Use CDN for API**: If your Vue application is making a lot of requests to an API, you might consider placing a CDN in front of that as well. CDNs can cache the responses of GET requests, which means that if two users make the same request, the CDN can return

the response from the cache instead of making a full round trip to your API server.

7. **Use Nuxt.js or Gridsome**: If you're building a server-side-rendered Vue.js application or a static site, using a framework like Nuxt.js or Gridsome can help you optimize for a CDN. These frameworks generate static HTML for each page of your app, which can be served directly from your CDN, improving load times.

It should be noted that these methods are often used interdependently and that the effectiveness of each may vary depending on the specifics of your application.

6.13   Discuss the intricacies of tree-shaking in a Vue application and how to ensure maximum efficiency.

Tree-shaking is a term commonly used in the JavaScript context to describe the removal of unused code. The term came from the metaphor of shaking a tree to remove dead leaves. In the context of a Vue.js application, tree shaking is de facto technique used to minimize the size of the application bundle and improve application load time and overall performance.

Tree shaking in Vue.js is often facilitated through build tools like Webpack or Module Bundlers like Rollup. That's possible because ECMAScript 2015's (ES6) module system allows static analysis of dependencies, making it easier to determine which parts of the codebase are not used.

The key to maximum efficiency in tree shaking is to ensure that the codebase imports only the pieces of code that are truly necessary. This could be achieved by using "named" or "specific" imports rather than importing the whole library or module. For example, instead of importing the entire lodash library, you can simply import the particular function you need:

```
// Instead of this...
import _ from 'lodash';

// Do this...
import { cloneDeep } from 'lodash';
```

Moreover, it is important that any code not used in production should be removed during the build process.

Also configuration of your bundler plays an important role in the efficiency of tree-shaking. For instance in Webpack, UglifyJS is used to remove the dead code(depends on Webpack's config) once it is marked as such. TerserPlugin is configured by setting optimization.minimizer and providing an instance of TerserPlugin.

```
const TerserPlugin = require('terser-webpack-plugin');

module.exports = {
  optimization: {
    minimizer: [new TerserPlugin()],
  },
};
```

Also, Babel has "presets-env", a preset that allows enabling transformations based on the environment and supports the tree shaking ability.

But it's not enough to rely solely on bundlers. To ensure that all dead code can be eliminated, you should minimize side effects in the application. Most third-party libraries specify in their package.json whether they have side effects. If you're publishing a library of your own to npm, then it's advised to add a "sideEffects" entry in your package.json file.

```
"sideEffects": false // for no module with side effects
"sideEffects": ["./side-effectful-file.js", "*.css"] // for specific side
    effect files
```

This tells the bundler whether to include the module with side effects into the final bundle, regardless if it exports used or unused code.

In conclusion, successful tree-shaking in Vue.js application involves careful management of imports, correct bundler configuration, effective handling of side effects, and mindful development practices to reduce the unnecessary code.

6.14   How would you handle dynamic module federation in a Vue application, especially in a micro-frontend architecture?

The concept of micro-frontend is to split a monolithic frontend into smaller, more manageable parts which can be developed and managed independently. To handle dynamic module federation in a Vue.js application, especially in a micro-frontend architecture, you'd follow steps as below:

1. **Setup Vue Project and Dependencies:** Create your Vue.js project and install needed dependencies like vue-router and loadable-components.

2. **Configure Module Federation Plugin:** Add and configure webpack's ModuleFederationPlugin in your webpack config file. This will expose specific parts of your application that can be consumed or used by other applications.

Example:

```
new ModuleFederationPlugin({
    name: 'app_name',
    library: { type: 'var', name: 'app_name' },
    filename: 'remoteEntry.js',
    remotes: {
        'app_name': 'app_name'
    },
    exposes: {
        './Component': './src/components/Component.vue',
    },
    shared: {
        vue: { eager: true },
        'vue-router': { eager: true }
    }
```

```
}),
```

3. **Set up Loadable-Components:** Use loadable-components to lazily load your federated modules at runtime dynamically. It allows you to split your codebase into multiple bundles which can then be loaded on demand or in parallel.

Example:

```
const LoadableComponent = loadable(() =>
    import('app_name/Component')
);

export default {
    components: {
        'loadable-component': LoadableComponent,
    },
};
```

4. **Configure vue-router:** Configure your vue-router to dynamically inject routes when they are needed. This gives you the flexibility to control how and when certain parts of your application are loaded and rendered.

Example:

```
import Vue from 'vue'
import Router from 'vue-router'
const loadableComponent = () =>
    import('app_name/Component')
Vue.use(Router)
export default new Router({
  routes: [
    {
      path: '/loadable-component',
      name: 'loadableComponent',
      component: loadableComponent
    }
  ]
})
```

5. **Use the Dynamic Component (Optional):** With the support of Vue's async component feature or Vue Router, we can load components / micro-apps dynamically. By using Vue's '<component :is="...">', we can decide what to use or render based on certain conditions.

Remember module federation allows for decoupling and isolation while sharing generic/common modules like libraries or components and fosters loosely coupled application architecture. You can continue to evolve your apps independently while re-using and sharing as necessary.

6.15 Describe strategies for ensuring zero downtime deployments in large-scale Vue applications.

Ensuring zero downtime deployments in large-scale Vue.js applications require careful planning and execution. Several best practices can help make this possible:

1. **Blue/Green Deployment:**

Blue/green deployment is a technique that reduces downtime and risk by running two identical production environments called Blue and Green. At any given time, only one of them is live (let's say Blue), with the live environment serving all production traffic. For the updates, the idle environment (Green) is updated, and once Green is tested and ready, the router switches all the traffic to the Green environment. Downtime is minimized, or in most cases eliminated, with Blue/Green deployment strategy.

2. **Feature Toggling:**

A feature toggle, also known as feature flag or feature switch, is a technique that allows software teams to toggle the visibility and use of features in an application. This can be used to gradually roll out features to subsets of users and revert back quickly in case of any unexpected issues.

3. **Scaling:**

Implement horizontal scaling solutions by adding more servers to handle increased load during the deployment phase.

4. **Monitoring:**

Set up proper application performance monitoring tools to catch any performance degradation early. This allows you to rollback any changes if required, without significant downtime.

5. **Automated Testing:**

Automate testing at various stages of your deployment pipeline to catch errors and address them before they impact live systems.

6. **Rolling Updates:**

Instead of updating all the instances of your application simultaneously, update them one at a time. This allows for a gradual deployment that doesn't take your entire application down if something goes wrong, which is especially useful in a microservices architecture.

7. **Canary Releases:**

A canary release is a technique to reduce the risk of introducing a new software version in production by slowly rolling out the change to a small subset of users before rolling it out to the entire infrastructure.

8. **Proper Documentation and Communication:**

Ensure there is a proper agreement on the deployment process among the involved teams (Developers, Testers, System Admins, Business Owners) before starting the process.

9. **Decoupling Your Services:**

Keep your services as decoupled as possible to ensure that an update to a single service does not need a complete overhaul of the whole application.

By implementing these strategies in a disciplined manner, you can significantly reduce and even eliminate the downtime during the deployment of Vue.js application updates. It's crucial to remember that every application is unique, with its own set of complexities, therefore, the strategies mentioned above should be adjusted based on the specific needs of your application.

6.16 How would you implement a custom directive in Vue that interacts with third-party DOM libraries?

Directives in Vue.js are an integral aspect of the framework. They allow you to directly edit the DOM in an instance of Vue. This includes creating a custom directive that interacts with a third-party DOM library. Here are the steps on how to achieve this:

1. First, you must register the custom directive using the global 'Vue.directive()' method or the local 'directives' option in a Vue component.

2. A directive has several hooks that can be used - 'bind', 'inserted', 'update', 'componentUpdated', and 'unbind'. Each hook corresponds to a particular point in the directive's lifecycle and can be used to define what the directive does at that point.

Here's an example of how to create a directive that interacts with jQuery UI's datepicker:

```
// Register the custom directive
Vue.directive('datepicker', {
  inserted: function(el) {
    $(el).datepicker({
      onSelect: function(date) {
        // When a date is selected, emit an event
        el.dispatchEvent(new Event('input', { bubbles: true }));
      }
    });
  },
  unbind: function(el) {
    // Destroy the datepicker instance when the directive is unbound
    $(el).datepicker('destroy');
```

```
    }
});
```

In this example, when the element is inserted into the DOM ('inserted'), we initialize the datepicker. Then, when a date is selected, we forcefully dispatch an 'input' event because jQuery UI does not do this by default. In Vue, an 'input' event updates the 'v-model' of an input element, so emitting this event in the 'select' callback ensures Vue's data is updated when a user selects a date. Lastly, if the directive is unbound from the element, ('unbind'), we clean up the datepicker instance to prevent memory leaks.

Then, in your Vue template, you would use your new directive like so:

```
<input v-datepicker v-model="pickedDate">
```

In this scenario, 'pickedDate' would be a data property on your Vue instance, and would be automatically updated whenever a user picks a date from the jQuery UI datepicker.

Please note that though manipulating the DOM directly from Vue is generally discouraged (it's often better to use Vue's built-in templating features and state management), it is necessary when integrating with third-party libraries that also interact directly with the DOM.

6.17   Discuss the potential challenges and solutions of integrating Vue with WebAssembly modules.

WebAssembly, or wasm, is a binary instruction format designed as a portable target for the compilation of high-level languages like C, C++, and Rust. Hence the integration of VueJS with the WebAssembly modules brings the capability for complex computations and enhanced performance in a Vuejs application.

However, integrating Vue.js with WebAssembly can potentially come up with several challenges. Here are a few of the common ones and the solutions to them:

1. **Language Barrier**: Given the current state of Webassembly, there is a language barrier as the best support for WebAssembly is using languages like C, C++, and Rust.

Solution: As it has gained more traction, there are now compilers available which will allow JavaScript developers to write their WebAssembly modules in TypeScript, which is very similar syntax-wise to Vue.js.

2. **Wasm module loading**: WebAssembly modules are not regular JavaScript modules and hence they might need special configuration in your build tools.

Solution: New 'wasmPackPlugin' in webpack like '@wasm-tool/wasm-pack-plugin' can be used. This will correctly load the WebAssembly module.

Example for using it with Webpack:

```
const WasmPackPlugin = require("@wasm-tool/wasm-pack-plugin");

module.exports = {
  plugins: [
    new WasmPackPlugin({
      crateDirectory: path.resolve(__dirname, ".")
    }),
  ]
};
```

3. **Synchronization**: JavaScript and WebAssembly run in the same event loop. Calls to a WebAssembly function will block JavaScript execution until the call is finished, so for long processes or infinite loops can seize the UI of a web app.

Solution: Use JavaScript Promises or the await/async functions. It helps to run the WebAssembly module asynchronously without blocking the UI.

Example:

```
async function loadWasmAndRun() {
  const wasmModule = await fetch('module.wasm');
  const { instance } = await WebAssembly.instantiateStreaming(wasmModule);
  instance.exports.wasmFunction();
}
loadWasmAndRun();
```

4. **DOM Access**: WebAssembly has no direct access to the DOM, it must go through JavaScript.

Solution: Functions will have to be written in JavaScript to manipulate the DOM and then called from within WebAssembly.

In the future, as WebAssembly continues to develop and gain support, it is expected that these challenges will become less pronounced or even completely irrelevant, making the integration of Vue.js and WebAssembly simpler and more seamless.

6.18   How would you handle cross-cutting concerns in a large Vue application, such as logging or analytics?

There are multiple ways to handle cross-cutting concerns like logging or analytics in a large Vue.js application. Two popular methods are using Middleware and Mixins.

1. Middleware: Middleware allows you to define custom functions that can run before rendering a layout or a page or even a group of pages. You can place your logging or analytics code inside these middleware to encapsulate the cross-concern logic.

For example:

```
export default function ({ isServer, req, redirect }) {
  console.log("I run before every route");
  // Add your analytics or logging code here...
}
```

In this case, the function will run before every route. You can add your analytics or logging code where indicated.

2. Mixins: In Vue.js, a mixin is a reusable chunk of code that can be incorporated into different Vue components. You can create a mixin that includes methods for logging or analytics, and then use that mixin in your various components.

Here's an example of a Mixin for Google Analytics:

```
export const googleAnalyticsMixin = {
  mounted() {
    if (this.$router) {
      this.$router.afterEach((to, from) => {
        ga('set', 'page', to.path);
        ga('send', 'pageview');
      });
    }
  }
}
```

This mixin can be used in any component by including it in the component's mixins array:

```
import { googleAnalyticsMixin } from './mixins';

export default {
  mixins: [googleAnalyticsMixin],
}
```

In this case, every time a route changes in a component that includes this mixin, a pageview will be sent to Google Analytics.

Another way to encapsulate cross-cutting concerns in larger Vue.js applications is with **Vue plugins**. A Vue plugin is an object that exposes an install method that will be called with the Vue constructor as the first argument. You can add global methods or properties, add components or directives, or inject some functionality into all components with a plugin.

In conclusion, Vue.js offers several ways to encapsulate cross-cutting concerns like logging and analytics. The method you choose will depend on the specifics of your project, but all methods aim to promote code reuse and a separation of concerns.

6.19   Describe the process of integrating advanced graphics libraries, like Three.js, into a Vue application.

Integrating an advanced graphics library like Three.js into a Vue application follows a distinct process. Here is a broad overview of the process:

1. **Install Three.js:**

Start by installing the Three.js library. You can install it via npm with the following command:

```
npm install three
```

2. **Import the Library:**

Once installed, you will need to import it into your Vue component. This can be done at the top of your script tag in your component file:

```
import * as THREE from 'three';
```

3. **Initialize Three.js within the Vue component:**

After this, you should initialize Three.js within the Vue component. You can do this within a method, or within Vue's mounted or created lifecycle hooks.

A simple example could look like this:

```
export default {
  mounted() {
    const scene = new THREE.Scene();
    const camera = new THREE.PerspectiveCamera( 75, window.innerWidth/window.
        innerHeight, 0.1, 1000 );
    const renderer = new THREE.WebGLRenderer();

    renderer.setSize(window.innerWidth, window.innerHeight);
    document.body.appendChild(renderer.domElement);

    // Add more Three.js code here...
  }
}
```

Here we're initializing a basic Three.js scene within the 'mounted()' lifecycle hook.

4. **Integrating with Vue's reactivity system:**

Any properties of the scene that should be reactive should be placed in Vue's data object so that Vue's reactivity system will know to update the scene when your data changes.

If you want to make any part of the Three.js scene reactive, you can do this by placing the scene, camera, and renderer directly in the data object and using Vue's computed or watcher features to react to changes.

5. **Cleaning up:**

It's good practice to remove any event listeners you attached or stop any animations when the component is unmounted or destroyed. This can be done inside Vue's 'beforeDestroy()' lifecycle hook.

```
beforeDestroy() {
  // remove event listeners, stop animations, etc.
  cancelAnimationFrame(this.animationFrame);
}
```

6. **Animation or Rendering Loop**

You'll also need an animation or rendering loop to constantly update the scene as needed. This is where you'd usually place the renderer's render function call. You would typically do this with the 'requestAnimationFrame' function in JavaScript.

```
methods: {
  animate() {
    this.animationFrame = requestAnimationFrame(this.animate);
    this.renderer.render(this.scene, this.camera);
  }
},
mounted() {
  this.animate();
}
```

This method 'animate' will recursively call itself before the next re-

paint to keep the scene updated. These are saved to 'this.animationFrame'
so it can be cancelled when the component is destroyed.

This is a brief overview. Depending on the complexity of your Three.js
scene, more integration may be necessary. Remember to keep track
of what is reactive and appropriately handle memory usage and performance.

6.20   How would you approach designing a Vue application for a decentralized web or blockchain-based platforms?

Designing a Vue.js application to deal with decentralized web or
blockchain-based platforms involves several specific considerations:

1. **Choosing an appropriate library for interaction with the blockchain**:
There are many libraries available, like web3.js for Ethereum or bitcore-
lib for Bitcoin to interact with blockchain. These libraries translate
the details of the blockchain protocol into an API that JavaScript can
interact with.

Example:

```
import Web3 from 'web3'
if (window.ethereum) {
    window.web3 = new Web3(window.ethereum)
    window.ethereum.enable()
}
```

2. **Modularize your components**: Create Vue components that
can handle blockchain-related tasks separately from the rest of your
application logic. This will lead to a cleaner and more maintainable
codebase.

3. **Integrate the blockchain into Vue's reactive state management**:
It's important to remember the blockchain represents a state just like
any other kind of data that a Vue application might manage, so it

should be integrated into Vue's state management (or similar state management library).

Here's a simple Vuex store configuration that integrates with web3.js:

```
const store = new Vuex.Store({
  state: {
    account: null,
    balance: null,
  },
  mutations: {
    setAccount (state, account) {
      state.account = account
    },
    setBalance (state, balance) {
      state.balance = balance
    },
  },
  actions: {
    async initialize({ commit }) {
      const accounts = await web3.eth.getAccounts()
      commit('setAccount', accounts[0])
      const balance = await web3.eth.getBalance(this.state.account)
      commit('setBalance', web3.utils.fromWei(balance, 'ether'))
    },
  }
})
```

4. **Design smart contracts**: You must design smart contracts to handle the business logic associated with your application. These contracts will operate in the blockchain and may include operations like token transfers or complex business rules.

5. **Testing**: Blockchain transactions are irreversible and can involve real-world assets. Therefore, testing is crucial. Libraries like Truffle provide a blockchain testing framework to automate tests for smart contracts.

6. **User Interface Considerations**: Blockchain transactions can take longer to complete than traditional web requests. UI components should be designed to handle these delays and provide appropriate feedback to the user. This could include loading spinners, progress bars, or other means of indicating that a transaction is in progress.

7. **Security Considerations**: Since blockchain involves value transfer and potentially sensitive operations, security is paramount. Vue

applications should be designed with best security practices in mind, like avoiding cross-site scripting vulnerabilities, implementing correct user authentication, and handling private keys with proper care.

8. **Error Handling**: Any application must handle errors effectively, and Vue.js is no exception to this. However, due to the nature and complexity of decentralized systems and blockchain technology, you should pay extra attention to error handling mechanisms.

These suggestions give a general overview of how to handle the architecture and design of a Vue.js application that interacts with a blockchain. An effective design will vary depending on the specific use case, so it's vital to consider all aspects of a project before settling on a design choice.

www.ingramcontent.com/pod-product-compliance
Lightning Source LLC
LaVergne TN
LVHW051334050326
832903LV00031B/3543